This is a "MUST REs owner. Howard Partrid) riches" story. In this bc he's used to go from zero to hero and more importantly, how YOU can too. You'll discover the "747 Business Model", the "Wheel of Life", the "FTI" syndrome and how to really do referral marketing. As someone who has worked with thousands of small business owners, this book gets my 5 Star rating.

David Frey - CEO,
MarketingBestPractices.com

I know of none other more equipped to write of a phenomenal life than Howard Partridge. Howard is a great example of hard work, determination, self-education, optimism and a heartfelt desire to share himself with others. His story is one of ingenuity, vision and persistence, told in the colorful flavor of his enthusiasm, transparency and joie de vivre. The phenomenal secrets he shares within these pages can change your life!

Laurie Magers,
Executive Assistant to Zig Ziglar

From the day I first met Howard Partridge, he began sharing his insights on building a "phenomenal business" and a "phenomenal life." *7 Secrets of a Phenomenal L.I.F.E.* is about to bless you with a powerful set of tips, tools, and solutions that will position you and your business for nothing less than phenomenal outcomes. If you are standing in a bookstore, *run* don't walk to the cash register, if you're buying this online click to the shopping cart *quickly* - this book is an essential investment in your future. Thanks Howard, for taking the time to cull this principled wisdom into such an effective resource!

Dr. Joseph A. Michelli
International Best-Selling Author of
*The Starbucks Experience*

Howard Partridge is a man of character and high integrity. In his book, *7 Secrets of a Phenomenal L.I.F.E,* Howard shares powerful insights that will radically change your life, but only if you take action. His combination of business and personal principles will give you tools so you too can live a phenomenal life! If you are serious about your success, then you must read this book!

Michelle Prince
Best-Selling Author, "Winning In Life Now"

I am so honored to have Howard as a friend and business associate. His energy and enthusiasm are contagious. The best part about Howard's book is that he comes alive on every page. It's like talking with him. You'll be inspired to create your own *phenomenal L.I.F.E.!*

Xo$, Ellen Rohr

Who better to teach us the *7 Secrets of a Phenomenal L.I.F.E.* than the phenomenal Howard Partridge? Scripture says that Jesus increased in wisdom (mentally), in stature (physically), and in favor with God (spiritually) and man (socially). This is more than a book. It's a uniquely insightful journey to self-discovery. After all, self-improvement follows self-discovery. In reading this book I was able to pinpoint a couple of "bottle necks" in my quest for success and was given the tools that I need to move forward. Don't leave here without it!

Eddie Smith,
Best-selling author,
copywriter, and writing coach

As Dad says, our goal is to achieve balanced success in every area of our life. *7 Secrets of a Phenomenal L.I.F.E.* shows you the Why and the How to achieving balanced success in your personal and business life. Howard Partridge has revolutionized my thinking on this concept more than anyone I have every met – except for Dad of course!

Tom Ziglar,
CEO and Proud Son of Zig Ziglar

Howard Partridge is a phenomenal person, so it's fitting he would write about how to have and enjoy a phenomenal life. This book shares his associations, his lessons, his ideas, and his structure. I urge you to read this book and implement the strategies and ideas he espouses so that you may become phenomenal too.

Jeffrey Gitomer,
author of *The Little Red Book of Selling*

If anyone knows about living life to the fullest, it is Howard Partridge. A wonderful book, from a wonderful leader!

Michael Gerber,
World's #1 Small Business Guru,
author of *The E-Myth* books

# 7 SECRETS *of a* PHENOMENAL L.I.F.E.

# 7 SECRETS *of a* PHENOMENAL L.I.F.E.

## Howard Partridge

**sound** wisdom
Shippensburg, PA

Sound Wisdom
167 Walnut Bottom Road
Shippensburg, PA 17257-0310

For more information on foreign distributors,
call 386-227-7814.

Reach us on the Internet: www.soundwisdom.com.

ISBN 13 TP: 978-1-937879-00-6

ISBN 13 Ebook: 978-1-937879-06-8

For Worldwide Distribution, Printed in the U.S.A.

1 2 3 4 5 6 7 8 / 16 15 14 13 12

# DEDICATION

To My Princess Denise.
Thank you for standing by me all these years.
I will always love you.
Your Knight in Shining Armor

# CONTENTS

# FOREWORD

*by Dr. William A. Beckham*

It has been a great blessing for me to walk with Howard through his phenomenal business and life journey. This has been one of those relationships where "iron sharpens iron" and both benefit. During this last decade-and-a-half, I have been thrilled to see others join his journey through his conferences and network.

The word "phenomenal" in this book is more than a catchy business name or a creative book title.

As used by Howard Partridge, the word is a life philosophy, a guiding principle and even a spiritual focus of life. Howard shares a great truth: Personal worth is a phenomenal product. This truth is the central concept of this book, of Howard's life and business.

In this book you can find the source of this "phenomenalness." David, the Psalmist and successful king, based his life and kingdom on this principle. "You (God) made him (man/humans) a little lower than the heavenly beings and crowned him with glory and honor. You made him ruler over the works of your hands; you put everything under his feet." (Psalms 8:5).

As stated in the Declaration of Independence, the inherent uniqueness of mankind is the foundational truth of the United States. "We hold these truths to be self-evident, that all men are created equal, that they are endowed by their Creator with certain unalienable Rights, that among these are Life, Liberty and the pursuit of Happiness."

This uniqueness (phenomenalness) is a wonderful gift bestowed upon us by the Creator. Jesus promised to "give life more abundantly." I believe Jesus would be comfortable using Howard's version: "I will give you phenomenal life." As you read this book, I hope you will accept the wonderful gift of your inherent worth as a special creation instead of trying to produce this quality by what you know, what you do, what you look like, where you are from, who your parents were or the size of your bank account. Author E. Stanley Jones wrote in his book, The Way, that there is a special Way of life that works (even in business) because it is built upon the universal principles of life and creation. "Nothing is so false than to say, 'Business is business,' for business that regards only itself and does not have regard to the moral universe sooner or later breaks itself upon that moral universe."

This book gives an integrated view of life that can help you discover the universal way of LIFE. Once we accept our inherent worth (our phenomenalness as a special creation of God) every aspect of life is transformed. Or, as Howard explains it, the Wheel of Life with its seven spokes begins to roll. Let me go ahead and give away Howard's secret...

This book is not about business, but it is really about you. In this book you can meet a phenomenal creation - YOU. Your first business is you, to know yourself and to respect yourself. You will be confronted with a phenomenal challenge - to become the person you were created to be. Therefore, your business vision and life goal is to fulfill your purpose and potential as a total person in your mind (what you think), in your emotions (what you feel) and in your body (how you treat yourself). If you choose, you will experience phenomenal change - freedom to be happy in every part of your life because of who you are, not what you do.

# ACKNOWLEDGEMENTS

I find this part of the book the most difficult to write. The reason? Because this book is about my life and I want to acknowledge everyone that has impacted my life. Of course that would take an entire book all by itself! I guess every author has the same frustration.

I suppose I could thank only those that had a part in writing and producing the book, or I could leave this section out altogether, but that wouldn't be right either, so I'll just pray I get it right.

Of course I have to thank God for saving me through Jesus in 1987. To my wonderful wife Denise for your amazing love, dedication and support through the struggles and successes. To my beautiful son Christian for helping me learn how to communicate better. To my little mama in Alabama for not giving us up for adoption and the tenacity I obviously inherited from you. My step father Hollis Odell. Even though he is passed away, I have to go on record to say that taking on 7 poor kids and putting up with me as long as he did was nothing less than saintly. And to my brothers Larry, James and Dennis and my two sisters Melanie and Gayle.

My real dad Earl Partridge who even though he left when I was only a year-old, did take me in at my rebellious prime - and that was probably due to my step-mother Marie Partridge who has always been proud to call me her son. To Georganne, Charmaine and Lee for accepting me as family.

To Jim Bardwell for being a believer from day one and being my best friend for life.

To my phenomenal team Michelle, Santiago & Elise, Daniel, Scott, Dago, Kenny, Jermaine, Kevin, Danny, Mary Ann, and all you outstanding techs!

To all of our clients, members, volunteers and industry leaders that continue to support our mission.

A special thanks to my phenomenal ambassadors, Luis Hernandez, John Browning, John Torres, John Braun, Dave DeBlander and Ralph Greco.

To my mentors, coaches and consultants Bill Beckham, Mark Ehrlich, Tom Ziglar, Ellen Rohr, Michelle Prince, Michael Gerber, Zig Ziglar, and John Maxwell.

To Nathan Martin with Sound Wisdom for believing in the message enough to publish it.

To Margaret Garrett for introducing me to Ziglar and for being a phenomenal person.

And finally to Laurie Magers, Executive Assistant to Zig Ziglar for keeping my voice while you did a super job on the first edit of the book.

# INTRODUCTION

## YOU Are a Phenomenal Product!

In 1998 I launched Phenomenal Products to help others improve their businesses. I asked my early mentor Bill Beckham to speak at one of my conferences. As he opened his presentation, he said to the audience...

"I'm sure Howard's products *are* phenomenal, but I'm here to tell you that *YOU* are a phenomenal product." He went on to say that all of us are created to *be* phenomenal, to *do* phenomenal things, and to *have* a phenomenal life.

Everyone wants a phenomenal life. Few live it out. Many people in America aren't truly happy with their lives. My goal for this book is to help you discover what a "phenomenal" life means to you, and how to have it.

### *If you own a business...*

If you own your own business, I wonder if you remember *why* you went into business for yourself to start with. Was it to make a lot of money? Or was it to be your own boss? To chart your own course – to have a little more "free time"?

Yeah, right!

*If you have been in business for a while, it probably feels more like a 7-day-a-week, 24-hour-a-day, J-O-B!*

The brutal reality of most small business owners' lives is you feel like a slave to the business, there's very little family time. The business consumes your mind 24/7. There's major stress, no real freedom, and you feel like you have a "job" rather than a business.

Your day is consumed putting out "brush fires."

In the following pages, I will show you how to break free from the demands of your everyday business and transform it into a predictable, profitable, turnkey business.

I've done it. And I've helped others do the same

## BE-DO-HAVE

Everyone wants to HAVE a phenomenal life. No one wants an "average" existence, but you may be settling for that. And that's a shame because if you live in America you live in the greatest country on earth where you can *have* whatever you want, *do* whatever you want and *be* the person you want to be.

If you own a business, I'm sure you want that business to be phenomenally successful. You may not know it yet, but owning a business in the United States puts you in a position of incredible influence. You can have more impact on your community than almost any other "institution."

This book is about HAVING the life you were created to have. It's about HAVING the business you are supposed to have. It's about HAVING the amount of money that is right for you. It's about HAVING the body you were created to have. It's about HAVING the knowledge you need to achieve your life goals. It's about HAVING phenomenal relationships with those around you. And finally, it's about having a phenomenal spiritual life.

My good friend Zig Ziglar says that in order to *HAVE* something different, you've got to *DO* something different. For example, if I want to HAVE more money, I've got to DO something different than I am doing now. It won't just "fall in my lap." If I want to HAVE better relationships, I have to DO something toward working on those relationships. If I want to HAVE a stronger, healthier body, I've got to DO something about it.

I think we get that.

### *What we may not understand is this...*

In order to consistently *DO* something different, you've got to *BE* something different. You've got to change. You've got to BECOME a different person than you are today.

That may sound a little scary to you, but I can tell you from personal experience that being willing to change is the key to having a phenomenal life.

I'm a different person than I was 20 years ago. I'm a different person than I was five years ago. I'm a different person than I was yesterday! Why? Because I have built a habit of learning. I have created the habit of change. Being willing to change has helped me live a life I only imagined. BE-coming a different person has helped me to DO different things which has allowed me to HAVE things in life that I never had before.

Don't get me wrong. I'm not trying to be someone I'm not. On the contrary, I'm learning who I really AM. Being aware of my habits, and what's working and what's not, and being willing to change, helps me grow, so that I can be a better person. I hope to be a different (better) person tomorrow based on what I learn today. I am learning who Howard Partridge is, what his purpose is, and what he was created to be – and more important – what he is called to do with his time on this planet.

If you are willing to BE-come a different person than you are now, you will be able to consistently DO different things than you are doing now, so that you can HAVE the things you want out of life. My goal is to help you accomplish that. And what you will learn is that you won't *consistently* DO things that are *inconsistent* with how you see yourself. I believe I learned this from Zig Ziglar, who gives Dr. Joyce Brothers the credit.

Zig talks a lot about self-image. He also says you are WHAT you are because of WHAT you put in your mind. Which means you can change what you are (and what you have) by changing what goes into your mind. So, we'll work on that. I hope that the following pages will convince you that you ARE a phenomenal product, created to DO phenomenal things, so that you can HAVE the phenomenal life you were created to have.

### From a "Welfare Throwaway Kid" to Living the "American Dream"

I'm originally from "L.A." (Lower Alabama!). I grew up on welfare in Mobile, Alabama. There were seven kids crammed into a little 600-square-foot shack. The roof on that house was so bad that every time it rained we had to get out the pots and pans to catch the leaks!

The house was on concrete blocks so there was no slab. It had a teeny-tiny shower (no bathtub) with barely enough room to turn around. One day my stepdad got in and it fell through to the ground! We propped it up with tree stumps, which created a gap between the shower floor and the rotten sheetrock. If the soap was dropped and bounced the wrong way, it would be *in the dirt*, *UNDER* the house!

### We *invented* soap-on-a-rope!

My little mama somehow fed us on a hundred dollars a month from the welfare department, and I still remember getting Christmas presents from the social workers. My real dad left when I was only a year old and I didn't get to meet him until I was 15. The only time I recall seeing him was at my grandfather's funeral. I must have been about five years old at the time.

As I stood on the sidewalk of the funeral home with my family, a long black limousine passed by and someone said "there's your father." The back window of the car was rolled down on his side and I got a glimpse of him. When he saw us, he placed a handkerchief over his face. He must have been so ashamed. Little did I know that he would become a significant part of my life later on.

How does a childhood like that usually turn out? You become a pot-smoking, hell-raising teenager. When I was 18, I got in a fight with my stepdad (who took on 7 kids and got us off of welfare) over my pot smoking habit. He told me not to come back until I "learned what pot would do to me".

This event turned out to be the best thing that ever happened to me. I had NO money. At the time, my sister was visiting my real dad in Houston (whom I had met only twice at this point). My friend and I scraped up $39.95 for a Greyhound Bus ticket to Houston. I wasn't really sure my dad would actually take me in, but I knew my sister would find a way.

When I stepped off that bus in downtown Houston, I literally had 25 cents in my pocket. No bank account. No credit card. That's all I had to my name. My real dad *was* there to pick me up and I lived with him and his new family (who I became very close to) for about a year. I made sure to patch things up back home in Alabama, too. Although both daddies are gone, I have a great relationship with both of my families today, for which I am very grateful.

After a few odd jobs in Houston, I became a professional waiter and worked in high end restaurants where we did flaming tableside cooking, wearing a tuxedo. I learned how to make a lot of great dishes at the table - steak Diane, pepper steak, Caesar salad dressing from scratch, hot spinach salad, bananas Foster, cherries jubilee, and many more. Setting stuff on fire *inside* was very cool indeed!

During my years as a waiter, I learned a great deal about the customer service experience, but I always wanted my own business. I've always been an entrepreneur at heart. As a kid, I cut grass, picked up pine cones, sold stuff door-to-door, and did anything I could to make money.

As I waited for the last table to leave each night, I scratched out business ideas on my waiter's pad. But I still had no money to speak of. I made just enough to pay the bills.

That's when I met my future wife. Denise Concetta Antoinette Pennella. Now, *that's* Italian! I went to New Jersey to get married to Denise and when you marry into an Italian family, you don't get wedding presents like dishes, toasters and blenders. Instead, you get CASH!

We got $3,000.00 in wedding money and while we were in New Jersey there was a friend of the family who was my age (23 at the time), tooling around in a little red Mercedes convertible. I said to myself *"I want to know what THAT guy does, and I want to know if it's LEGAL!"*

Turns out he owned a business. So, as soon as I got back to Houston, I spent all of our wedding money to start a business. My wife was really thrilled about that, let me tell you!

So, I started my first business out of the trunk of my car. I still own that business today. Over 13 long years I got it up to about $30k per month. I was making good money, but I had become a slave to the business. Everything revolved around me. I couldn't go on vacation without the appointment book or spending much of the vacation solving problems over the phone.

If you're a small business owner and you have been in business for awhile, you know what I mean.

### *Two Big Secrets that Changed My Life Forever...*

My mentor Bill Beckham would come to my office about once a week to talk and pray with me. As he observed how involved I had to be in every little detail of the business, and how dependent it was on me, he recommended I read *The E-Myth Revisited* by Michael Gerber.

That book changed my business and my life forever.

After reading *The E-Myth*, I took a week off and went to my favorite place in the world, Destin, Florida, and sat on the beach and re-created my future. The first secret I learned was how to build a turnkey business – one that operates just as well *without* you as it does *with* you. I learned how to work *on* the business instead of just *in* it as *The E-Myth* says.

The second secret I learned (also from *The E-Myth*) is that the only reason your business exists is to help you achieve your LIFE GOALS. You went into business for yourself because you had a dream of having more time for your family – a dream of doing WHAT you want WHEN you want. Instead, you sometimes feel like a slave to the business.

That's what I felt like. I was literally a prisoner of my own making. Don't get me wrong, I LOVED serving my customers and doing the technical work of the business, but now I saw a different picture. I saw that I could have a turnkey business.

I recruited two friendly competitors to join my team and we began working on our systems. That business skyrocketed to almost $3 million per year! And the best part is that it *is* turnkey, which means I don't have to be involved in the day-to-day operations. I have a staff of 27 that runs my companies for me.

In 1998, I began teaching my systems to other business owners through information products, seminars and coaching. As it turns out, I was speaking at the same convention as Michael Gerber (author of the book that changed my life – *The E-Myth Revisited*). The seminar promoter arranged for us to meet over breakfast.

Since that breakfast meeting in Las Vegas, Michael has not only presented at my live events, he has become a great friend and mentor to me. I talk to him several times a year and I will always be grateful to him for changing my business life. I love Michael and he is a brilliant, incredibly gifted man.

Since that time I have had partners, bought and sold businesses, and even started a franchise operation. My live events have included world famous American legend Zig Ziglar, best-selling authors

Tamara Lowe (who runs Get Motivated!, the largest business seminars in the world), Bob Burg (author of *Endless Referrals* and *The Go-Giver*), Dr. Joseph A. Michelli (author of *The Starbucks Experience*), and others.

And I have been endorsed by Dr. John C. Maxwell, the #1 leadership expert in the world.

I am especially grateful for my relationship with the Ziglar Corporation. I have been blessed to not only share the stage with Zig, and to be featured on their live webcasts, but to enjoy a close personal relationship with the entire Ziglar family and team. And I recently launched their very first coaching program for business owners.

Some years ago, when I still had a very small business and a very small staff, I was part of a local industry group that met every week to talk about ways to improve our businesses. There were about a dozen people that met every Monday morning. They complained about the economy and how customers wouldn't pay their price. They had what Zig calls "stinkin'-thinkin'" and they needed a "check-up from the neck up"!

Some of them were wearing cut-off blue jeans, flip-flops and hadn't shaved, and they wondered why they didn't have much business. I strolled in carrying a briefcase, in a sport coat and tie, wearing a positive attitude. They literally laughed at me and said, *"Who do you think you are, Zig Ziglar or somebody?"!*

The funny thing is I did not know Zig Ziglar at the time. Little did they know, they were speaking prophecy!

# 1

## IT'S A PHENOMENAL L.I.F.E.

In the classic film *It's a Wonderful Life,* Jimmy Stewart's bank had all but collapsed and he was on the verge of jumping off a bridge to end his life. Little did he know that he had a guardian angel assigned to him and many wonderful people that loved him and cared about him, regardless of the circumstances. He didn't realize the difference he had made in other's lives.

We live in a fallen world. We never know what trial we may face tomorrow. Learning to make the best of the circumstances we face is one of the first keys to living a phenomenally successful life.

One of my best friends was Ray Davis. Ray suffered from MS for many years and in the last 10 years of his life he couldn't even get out of bed. His arms and legs were stiffened in place by the disease. Even his fingers were permanently gnarled and inflexible. As he lay there in constant, agonizing pain, he could move only his lips. If you didn't know Ray well like I did, you couldn't understand his garbled, slurred speech. I was glad that I could understand him because Ray's purpose was to encourage everyone who came to his bedside.

Regardless of his condition, he wanted to know about *your* life and how *you* were doing. He always glorified God and was so thankful for the little things. He was always hopeful for the future. Maybe there would be a miracle break-through drug. Maybe God would heal him. Maybe he would be able to move his fingers just a *little* bit today. My "problems" seemed small after leaving Ray's bedside. I was grateful just to be able to walk to my car.

The last time I saw Ray alive was in the hospital. I was the only one there and the room was dark. A nurse had come into the room and Ray wanted to pray for her. On his death bed, in the last hours of his life, his concern was for someone he didn't even know!

Ray used what he had. He may not have been able to help anyone physically, but he was able to make a difference with what he *did* have: His heart. And his mind.

I have a picture of an African slave I took out of a magazine. Judging by the date of the photograph and the age of the man (who appeared to be over 70), he was most likely plucked from his freedom by white foreigners and put on a slave ship. Though I cannot pretend to know what this man experienced, I *do* know that there are two places that NO ONE can touch except him and God, and those two places are his heart and his mind.

I have that picture to remind me that I have no problems!

History is littered with people who endured nightmarish atrocities, but emerged with a sense of freedom, purpose and joy. The first step to living a phenomenally successful life is to *not* live out of your circumstances. Begin to focus on what you *do* have, rather than what you *don't* have. This was hard for me because I have been blessed with many comforts in life. Don't get me wrong, my wife and I work hard for what we have. But I can get too focused on how things should be, rather than just being grateful for what I have.

## *Gratitude*

You may not feel that you have much to be grateful for. Maybe you have tremendous problems. Maybe your future doesn't look bright. I want to introduce you to a mental process that I think will serve you well. It has not come easily for me, but I now realize that when I use it, I am able to focus on what is truly important.

Some years ago I was introduced to a man by the name of Jerry Wiles. Jerry has authored a number of books and has a syndicated radio show. He serves as the *president emeritus* of Living Water International. LWI drills wells across the world in places where clean drinking water isn't available. I learned from them that almost *one billion people* on the planet don't have access to clean drinking water! I discovered that this is the #1 killer on earth!

How is that possible? That's 20% of the planet! I quickly learned to be more grateful for what I have. It just so happens that as I write this piece we have no water in my house because of a deep freeze last night. Although I live in a beautiful home, we are on a water well which froze during the night.

During Hurricane Ike we were without power for three weeks. The water well is electric, so we had no running water. After several days, with the help of a friend, we got a generator hooked up. But before that it was sponge baths by candlelight, and that was just a little less comfortable than I'm used to. To top it off, it happened to be my birthday!

That experience taught me to be grateful for the little things. If you live in America, you have so much to be grateful for. Being able to just flip a switch for light, water and warmth. Having garbage service. The freedom to worship. The freedom to pursue your dreams.

The freedom to grow a PHENOMENAL business that will take you places you never dreamed possible and to bless more people than you could ever imagine.

Zig Ziglar says:

*Of all the "attitudes" we can acquire, surely the attitude of gratitude is the most important and by far the most life-changing.*

Be grateful for the little things and your mind and heart will be opened to new possibilities for your life. Otherwise, you will be stuck in your own prison of pity.

Every day when we wake up, we have a *choice* of what to focus on. When you wake up, and your "problems" begin to fill your mind, or you begin to become overwhelmed with the duties required for today, stop and replace those thoughts with gratefulness. Begin to think about what you *do* have. Thank God for your freedom. Thank God for everything you have in all areas of your life. Be grateful for the little things and you will see your attitude begin to change.

## *Embrace the Struggle*

For years Zig Ziglar taught us to *respond* to circumstances rather than *react* to them. In other words, make the best out of what you are dealt in life. Many people scoffed at Zig because "he had it all." A world-famous speaker and author. Millions of fans. Of course he's going to be positive!

But one night he fell down the stairs in his home and nearly killed himself. The fall resulted in a terrible case of vertigo and short-term memory loss. Seemingly everything that made Zig who he was – his animated speeches, his positive attitude, his sharp wit – all put to the test. Would he complain? Would he use it as an excuse to quit? Would he start a Zig Ziglar pity party?

No way! Instead, he proved his message by doing the best he could with the situation. He continued to travel and continued to inspire. And he wrote a book about it with his daughter, Julie Ziglar Norman.

*Embrace the Struggle* guides the reader through the process of not only overcoming the struggle, but embracing it. Many times the worst things that happen to us eventually become the best things as they bring unexpected blessings.

In some ways I think his short-term memory loss helped the audience. At one of my events, he and Julie were on my stage. After repeating how important marriage was for the sixth time, one of my attendees finally "got it." He rushed out of the room, called his girlfriend and asked her to marry him! Sometimes men need to hear something six times before it sinks in!

Six months later the couple married (at my live seminar, which was pretty unique!). Several of us went on a fabulous Costa Rican adventure afterwards. While there, he showed me a personal letter he had received from Zig encouraging their marriage.

### *Remember Helen Keller*

Helen Keller was deaf, dumb AND blind! Yet she became an author, speaker, and American legend. How did she do it? She had vision. She also had a teacher. I'll get to that in a moment. *The first and most important key to having a phenomenal life is a strong, compelling VISION.* Helen Keller said, "The only thing worse than being blind is having sight but no vision."

This does NOT mean that you will have everything figured out. It just means that you will have a sense of freedom in your life because you have thought about what kind of life you want to live. What does that look like?

I personally believe that deep down, everyone has a dream. They may not be able to articulate it, and you may not even be able to see that you have a dream. But you do. There *is* an image of the kind of person you want to be. There is an image of the kind of life you want to live. The trouble is that we have forgotten how to dream.

Last year I had the pleasure of interviewing Rudy Ruettiger, the real guy that the movie *Rudy* was about. Rudy had a dream to play football for Notre Dame. He was to small, too slow, and not strong enough. He wasn't even smart enough to get into Notre Dame, but he never gave up on his dream and he *did* go to Notre Dame, and he *did* get on the team. And you probably know the story, he did get to play the final game of the season and he sacked the quarterback!

During the interview, Rudy said that typically children are encouraged to dream until fifth grade, when all of a sudden they are told they need an education to be successful and their dreams are squashed. We have forgotten how to dream.

You may not find your dream as a result of this book, but I hope to help you develop a simple vision for your life. A clear picture of who you are and what you want out of life is critical to having a phenomenally successful life.

If you are a business owner, having a vision for your life is critical for building the right kind of business. We usually get that backwards. We usually build the business without considering the impact on our lives. Remember that the only reason your business exists is to help you achieve your *life goals*. There is no other reason.

What I mean by *life goals* is what you want your life to look like. The vision for your life. If you aren't clear about what you want out of life, you won't build the kind of business that will serve you well. Your business has a huge impact on your personal life.

If you don't have a compelling vision for your life, you won't do the things you need to do and you won't become the person you want to become.

In other words, if I don't even know *what* I want to *have*, how can I know what to *do*? And if I don't know what I am supposed to do each day, how in the world can I know what kind of person I need to *be*?

So, it all starts with the dream. The vision. The vision for your L.I.F.E.

*I created an acronym*
*for L.I.F.E.*
*that goes like this...*

Living

In

Freedom

Everyday

The kind of freedom I'm talking about here is the freedom of the mind. A freedom in your heart. To "find yourself," so to speak. To really know that you are living the life that you are called to live.

There is a sense of freedom when you know you are becoming the person you are supposed to be. Everyone wants to be happy. Everyone wants to feel that sense of freedom. I don't think you ever "arrive," and you want to always be growing, but knowing you are on the right track is very freeing.

Maybe the life you are living isn't the life you want. Maybe you haven't a clue about how to begin living a different life. Maybe you've never even thought about it. My hope is that this book will help you discover the groove you are called to and that it will help you get on the right track.

Everyone wants to be happy. Everyone wants to be successful. Does "living in freedom" every day mean that you won't have problems? No. Does it mean every day will be phenomenal? Well, Zig says if you don't think every day is a good day, try missing one!

Speaking of Zig Ziglar, his definition of success is "having a balanced life." To demonstrate this, he uses a tool called the Wheel of Life. You may be familiar with it. I have found it to be very helpful.

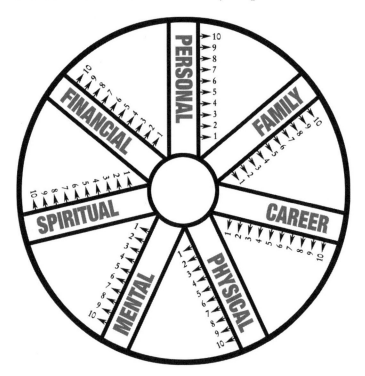

## *There are 7 spokes on the Wheel of Life....*

1.  *Personal* – Your own dreams, aspirations, hobbies and goals. Your social activity (as much as it depends on you). Basically your lifestyle.

2.  *Financial* – Your income, your financial position, and what you do with your money.

3.  *Career* – Your work, your role in your job or business and what that means to you and those around you, as well as the contribution to the world it represents.

4.  *Mental* – Your knowledge, your mental growth, the things that occupy your mind. This includes things you want to learn.

5.  *Physical* – Your physical condition (as much as it depends on you) - your eating habits, exercise, addictions, etc.

6.  *Family* – Your relationship with family members (as much as it depends on you), and what kind of person you want to be in relationship to family members. Remember, you cannot change anyone, but if you change yourself, you have a much better chance of someone else changing as a result of your example.

7. *Spiritual* – Your relationship with God (as much as it depends on you). What kind of faith member is ideal? What is your role in that?

Take a few moments to think about each "spoke" on the wheel. How do you feel about where you are in each area right now? Rate that area in your life on a scale of 1-10, 1 being poor and 10 being phenomenal. Circle the number that best describes how you feel about that area in your life, based on your ideal vision. Be honest with yourself.

Once you have circled a number on each spoke, connect the dots with a line. You will immediately see whether your life is balanced or not. Do you have a flat tire? When your wheel isn't balanced, the road of life is pretty bumpy.

It may even be painful to think about some of these areas. This is normal, and it's okay. I'll try to help you face some of the challenges you see. I hope to help you move those areas up little by little until you not only know you are a phenomenal product, but you feel it, too!

## *Life out of balance*

Would you agree that if I make a lot of money but my family life is messed up, I'm not living a phenomenally successful life? What if I'm a hugely "spiritual" person, but I'm deeply in debt? Doesn't really work, does it? Each of the areas affects the other. You may feel that you can't be a "borderline-eleven" in every area, but I'm here to tell you that you CAN!

And if you don't believe that, can I ask you which area in your life *shouldn't* be phenomenal? Does it mean you should be "filthy rich"? After all, if I'm saying you should be phenomenal in every area of life, doesn't that include financial, too? Yes, it does, but when you get to the chapter on *How to Make Phenomenal Money*, you might be surprised at what I have to say.

Now that you have completed the wheel on how you feel about your life now, let's do a very exciting exercise.

Using the same wheel, now let's set some goals. Let's create a *vision* for your life. I like to start with a 90-day time period. Think about the areas that need to be balanced. Imagine your life 90 days from now. What are some realistic goals you could set in each of those areas? Ignore any negative thoughts right now. Instead, assume that you can overcome any challenge that might get in your way. If there were *no* obstacles, what numbers could you realistically set on the wheel?

For example…when I first did the wheel, I put down a "2" on family because my relationship with my son wasn't the greatest at the time. It was far from phenomenal, let me tell you! But I set a goal to move it up. Today, I would rate it at a 9. And remember that I am only rating it based on my part in the relationship. Even if the other person never responds, you can eventually give yourself a 10 if you have truly done everything possible on your end. Only you know if you have or not. Only you and God can be the judge of that.

Developing a vision for your life, and focusing on that vision daily, is the first and most important key.

*The only thing worse than being blind is having sight but no vision.* —Helen Keller

When you have a compelling vision for your life – one that is incredibly inspiring – you will have the energy to fight through difficult circumstances.

*Strong vision endures heavy crosswinds*
                                        —Unknown

Another wonderful exercise is to describe your perfect day. You are the spiritual person you are called to be. You are responding and leading in your family in a way that is fulfilling. You are in the best physical shape you can be. Your mind is sharp. Money is not an issue, and you are doing what you love. You are spending time with friends, and you are pursuing your passion in life.

## *What would that look like for you?*

Many people find that a "vision board" is helpful. Get a bulletin board or poster board, a wall, mirror or any place that you will see every day. Find pictures that inspire you. A friend of mine was recently with some fighter pilots and noticed that each of them had a picture of their family on the instrument panel. When he asked why, they all responded that the pictures reminded them what they were fighting for.

## *What are you fighting for?*

Your vision must be compelling. It must be inspiring. It must energize you. And you must be willing to put your dream to the test. Recently I met the world-renowned John C. Maxwell and joined his training team as a founding member. At the time he was promoting his book, *Put Your Dream to the Test.* It has 10 important questions to ask yourself about your dream. The fact that you don't have a compelling vision for your life is a reflection of what you are actually *getting* out of life.

I believe that developing a *vision* for your L.I.F.E. is the most important thing you can possibly do. The reason is that your actions follow your vision. Your actions determine your destination.

If you don't really know what you want out of L.I.F.E., use the Wheel of Life and ask yourself these three questions in <u>each area</u> of the wheel.

1. *WHAT do I want my life to look like in this area?* (remember — as much as it depends on you)

2. *WHY do I want this?* (this is what will drive you, so it must be a big WHY)

3. *HOW can I get there?* (what are some possible strategies you can use to make this a reality in your life?)

You will most likely need some outside input. Get input from your mentors, coaches and family members. So the first step to living a phenomenally successful life is to think about what you want your life to look like in these seven areas.

Develop a VISION for your life. Instead of living out of the circumstances, you live out of the beautiful, freeing, inspiring vision instead. This keeps you focused on moving forward rather than getting down about what you don't have right now. Remember that there are many others who are worse off than you. And remember, this doesn't mean you won't have problems. It just means that you will have a compelling vision that will help you overcome the challenges with more grace and success.

## F.T.I.

The next step is to ACT on your dream. So often we get lots of ideas, but we fail to *implement*. We come up with business plans we never implement. We think we have good intentions, but we never seem to "get there." **I often say the number one reason small business owners don't grow (or do as well as they could) is because of F.T.I. (Failure To Implement).**

You know what to do and how to do it, but you still don't do it. The reason? You don't have a strong enough *vision*. You don't truly *believe* that it will happen. If you did, you would implement.

> *Vision without action is a daydream.*
> *Action without vision is a nightmare.*
> —Japanese Proverb

So, vision without action is only a daydream. But where most people live is *action* without vision. You simply react to the circumstances of the day. Your day is consumed putting out "brush-fires" but you never seem to get traction. This is because your actions are not tied to a strong vision. When you know where you are going and you believe it will be phenomenal, you will begin to do the hard stuff you need to do.

## The DREAM TEAM

You need people around you to help you develop your dream and to keep you accountable to live out the life you are supposed to live. Your Dream Team consists of people you want to model your life after as well as people who can support you.

When I say "model," I don't mean copy. One of the excellent coaching processes I have used is The Growth Coach Strategic Planning Process®. My good friend Glenn Smith owns the franchise in Houston. In their planner there is a statement that says...

*"I will model the mindset, strategies and habits of the following person:"*

Modeling means you respect their values. One of the names that has occupied that space on my planner is Bill Beckham. He was one of my earliest mentors. He is one of the wisest men I know. He is also the man who introduced me to *The E-Myth* book and the one who declared to my audience "YOU are a PHENOMENAL PRODUCT!" He is an incredible visionary and he has an amazing, prophetic insight that cuts right to the root issue when he is mentoring others. Another name that has appeared on that line is Zig Ziglar. If I can maintain just a fraction of the positive attitude that man has, I'll be pretty doggone phenomenal!

I live by the principle of *finding the people who have already done what I want to do* and learning from them. Contact those you identify with and find out if they will mentor you. Most successful people are happy to help you because that's how they got to where they are. If the person is a paid coach or consultant, pay their fee or find a way to offer appropriate value. Join their programs and buy their products. Support them and help them.

Mentors will help you discover your unique and phenomenal abilities and that will change your life forever, so it's worth whatever you invest. I believe that most people need others to see them from the outside. I know I do. I am so grateful to all of those who have encouraged me because they saw my talent and calling. They saw my potential when I couldn't see it.

## *Having a mentor clears up the confusion*
## —Rudy Ruettiger

When I interviewed Rudy at the Ziglar studio, he said that we all suffer from "goofy thinking" and that we have a lot of confusion. He made a big point of getting mentors to help us clear things up. All of us need mentors, coaches, consultants, our spouse and others in our lives that can see things from the outside.

Spend time with people who have your best interests at heart. People who will encourage you, inspire you and love you enough to challenge you. You need a DREAM TEAM.

My Dream Team includes coaches, consultants, mentors, friends, associates, staff members, and my wife, of course. My nephew helped me name Phenomenal Products when he was about 15. I'm not sure how we came up with it, but we were brainstorming one day and the word *phenomenal* popped out. A teenager that didn't really have a lot going for him at the time.

The original idea for Phenomenal Products came late one night on a long, dark stretch of Texas highway. One of my employees and I were driving to the beach at South Padre Island. I was doing some association work at the time and we began to talk about how cool it would be to have some products that would help small business owners.

Before too long I had a couple of manuals, some CDs, and some live workshops. Now you are reading my first book! It has been an incredible ride, but the seed was planted gnawing on beef jerky and sipping a Coke driving down the road.

My Dream Team encourages me to think bigger, and they also caution me if they sense that our brand or reputation may be affected.

*If you don't value people, you de-value people.*
## —Dr. John C. Maxwell

All of business and all of life is about relationships. Your relationship with clients, employees, co-workers, vendors, and family members. Your relationship with God and your relationship with yourself. How you *value* others will determine how you will *act* toward them. Zig Ziglar's most famous quote, and his personal favorite to this day is…

*"You can have everything in life you want, if you will just help enough other people get what they want."* —Zig Ziglar

During the first time I interviewed him on video I told him that he "stole" that quote from Jesus, because Jesus said...

*"Give and it will be given back to you in good measure, pressed down, shaken together and running over."* —Jesus

Zig just laughed and said, "Well, I know Him personally, so I think that'll be all right!" What wit!

## What is *your* calling?

I believe that God created each one of us for a specific purpose. Each one of us has a post in life, and each of us has a certain gifting and calling. Your mentors, coaches, and consultants will help you discover that. Your Dream Team will help you get there.

Once you have set some goals in each of the areas of your life, and thought about how you will get there, you will develop an action list. A set of first steps that you must do in order to live out the life you want. For example, when I made the decision to write this book, I established a goal of investing one hour a day, six days a week until I finished it.

I have used this same approach to complete other projects in the past. For example, when I started Phenomenal Products, my first order of business was to write some manuals. I got up every day around four a.m. and invested two to three hours a day to complete the manuals.

Take action NOW on your goals and dreams.

# 2

# THINK AND GROW PHENOMENALLY SUCCESSFUL

Over a century ago, a man by the name of Napoleon Hill published a book titled *Think and Grow Rich*. The book was the result of a massive study by Hill of 500 of the most successful people in the country.

The bottom line of the study and the focus of the book is that the difference between highly successful people and those who aren't is how they *think*. The size and depth of your thinking determines your success. And remember, we're not talking about just money here - we're talking about a balanced life. We're talking about success in *all* areas of life.

Those that Hill studied may or may not have had success in all areas and may or may not have had balanced lives. They were certainly rich. All of them. However, the power of using the phenomenal mind they had could have been used in all seven areas, not just one.

And that's the point - that you were given a phenomenal mind that has so much potential, few people on the planet use it to the level that is possible. How many people do you know that have an enormous bank of useless knowledge about trivia, but don't have any clue about how to make money? By the same token, how many mega-rich people are there in this world that are so emotionally messed up that they end up committing suicide, murder or overdosing?

So, thinking to grow phenomenally successful is not just about being rich monetarily. It's about thinking to become successful in *all* areas of life. The value of *Think and Grow Rich* is to understand how to use the wonderful mind God gave us. Let me go on record to say that I don't agree with everything Napoleon Hill wrote in that book. Especially some of the "spiritual" things. However, if you can be nonreligious for a moment and begin to understand how to use your mind more effectively, I'm convinced you will be much farther down the road to being phenomenally successful.

And by the way, if you are a true Christian (one who believes that the Holy Spirit lives inside of you and you are born-again), where is *your* battle? It's in your mind. Continuing to focus on who you are in Christ has a huge impact.

When you came to know Christ, you had to repent of your own independence and trust God through Jesus Christ. What does the word *repent* mean? To change your *mind*. Now I believe there is a spiritual revelation that takes place and salvation is not just a calculated decision based on information; but how many people get a vision from God and still don't repent? So, the Spirit and the mind work together.

## *The focus of this chapter is two-fold...*

1.  To share how I believe the mind works.

2.  To share some thinking strategies and habits that have helped me realize some of my biggest dreams in life, and how they will help you, too.

I'm not just going to tell you to think big or to dream big, I'm going to show you how. I'm going to do my best to convince you to spend more time *thinking* because the size of your success depends on the depth and quality of your thinking.

You've probably heard that your results are determined by your actions and your actions are determined by your attitude and your attitude is determined by your belief and your belief is shaped by your thinking. So it all starts with thinking. I like to add praying to that because I never want to leave the phenomenal God factor out of the equation.

The battle is in the mind and *for* your mind. We'll also look at how emotion wins over mind and how to begin having some victory over your impulses, limiting belief systems, and even addictions.

### *Who do you think you are?*

In the introduction, I shared how a group of negative guys laughed at me and said, "Who do you think you are, Zig Ziglar or somebody?" Zig teaches that a poor self-image is what holds human beings back from success. What we truly believe about ourselves limits our potential because every human acts or doesn't act based on how we see ourselves.

You will take action based on the *picture* you see in your mind. So you must change the picture if you want to change your results. For over three decades, people flocked to Dallas time and again for Zig's *Born To Win* seminar. The basis of *Born To Win* is that "You are what you are because of *what* you put into your mind and you can change what you are by changing *what* you put into your mind."

You may not even be aware of your limiting thoughts because they are often hidden. They are hidden in our "conditioned identity." "This is just who I am" is often the motto. Your *conditioned identity* is the identity you have accepted based on the *conditioning* you have received over a lifetime.

## *Five Steps to Changing Your Habits*

Years ago, I learned a process of understanding how habits and values change from a man by the name of Dr. Ralph Neighbor, Jr., a brilliant and gifted man who has pioneered the cell church movement worldwide. Along with my very wise mentor, Mr. Bill Beckham, I learned a great deal about human behavior from Dr. Neighbor. This is also where I got my start with small group learning.

Before sharing these five important steps, let me also point out something I learned from a couple by the name of Annabelle and Bill Gillham...

As we know, the human is made up of spirit, soul and body. The soul is made up of three parts: the mind, will, and emotion. Through our conditioning over our lifetime, our emotions (or lack of) create powerful grooves in our mind. Gillham calls them "green highways." Through this conditioning, we get our assumed identity (the picture I was talking about a moment ago). That's why I call it a *conditioned identity,* because it is based on our conditioning over time and is not a result of truth.

As I write this little piece, I'm on a small Puerto Rican island. Yesterday I went to play basketball at an outside court in the middle of town. The court was packed with children having playtime. Almost all the kids were fighting or struggling over something, it seemed. One kid slapped another kid across the face. Another was protecting the other boys. As I observed these playground kids, I couldn't help but imagine what emotional green highways were being cut in their soul.

Emotions are very powerful and create habits through these deep grooves. Your mind is telling you one thing (like *don't eat that ice cream or you'll get fat!*) and your emotion is screaming *I want ice cream!* Mind is telling you one thing and emotion is pulling the opposite direction. Gillham declares that one of them will eventually settle the battle...

The "big boss" that ultimately settles the debate is named *will*. *Mind, will* and *emotion*. Mind says one thing; emotion says another, but will always wins.

Think of eating habits for a moment. In my emotions I want ice cream. But I'm conflicted because I want to lose weight. My mind says "NO!" Yet my emotions continue to pull (along with the green highways I have developed in my fleshly body). In order for the mind to really win this fight, emotions have to change and habits have to change. The following five steps reveal what you experience as you go through the process of changing value systems. It has been helpful for me to understand the process so that I can see myself all the way through to the new habits that will give me the results I want.

(Another reason I want to share this is because of what my members have shared with me: Out of all the massive material I have produced over almost a decade and a half, I have probably gotten more positive feedback on the audio recordings I have done about these steps called *5 Steps to BE-Coming a Phenomenally Successful Person*. I hope it has the same impact for you.)

## *Step 1: Self-Awareness*

Because of our emotional conditioning, we begin by being unaware of what's happening in our soul (mind, will and emotion). We must begin by stepping outside of ourselves and becoming AWARE. Becoming *aware* of your actions. Becoming *aware* of your thoughts. Becoming *aware* of your habits. Remember, if you aren't getting the result you want, it's because of the action you have taken (or not). It doesn't happen by accident. It is a focused effort.

For most of us it takes others to help us see who we really are and what our potential is. I'm so grateful to those in my life that have helped me discover my gifts and those who continue to do so today. I believe that we all need edification and that each one of us has a role to build others up and encourage one another. Zig says, "Encouragement is the fuel that hope runs on." Please understand I am not talking about encouraging selfish ambition, self-destructive habits, or enablement. On the contrary, helping others create the awareness that we *all* need to become the person we are called to be.

We must face reality while maintaining our faith. Face the reality that I'm not living the life I am called to live and it's because I am sticking my head in the sand. It's not because of the economy or what another person is or isn't doing. It's all about WHO I believe I am and WHAT I'm supposed to be doing.

Self-awareness is nothing more than a muse if there isn't a greater purpose behind it. Maybe at this point all you know is that you want to BE a better person. That's a start. *Why* do you want to be a better person? For what purpose? Maybe you want be more effective? Why?

A great "self-coaching" exercise is to think about what you want and ask yourself *why* you want it. When you get the answer, ask yourself the same question about that answer. Continue asking why behind each question until you've completely exhausted your mind. It is quite annoying if you aren't used to it!

This exercise is also used to identify fear (which I will deal with in a moment). Here's an example...I was coaching a member who was fearful of making referral source calls. "What's the fear behind that?" I asked.

"They won't like me."

"And the fear behind that?"

"They won't refer me."

"The fear behind that?" I pressed.

"I won't get any business."

"And that means?" I continued to lead.

"Then I won't be able to feed my kids!" she exclaimed.

Can you see how the fear of not being able to feed her kids was driving this all along? Now, I'm no psychologist or therapist, but a basic working knowledge of this can really help! The TRUTH in this case is that she wasn't getting any business from these referral sources anyway (and her kids were eating regularly). Knowing what I know about referral marketing, I would be more fearful of NOT making the calls!

Creating a habit of becoming aware of what you are doing and why you are doing it is the first step to changing your thinking, which in turn shapes your beliefs. You may already know what you believe and why, but you aren't living out the life you have envisioned. Stopping yourself in your tracks to check your actions and your thoughts will help you get started.

One of the tools I like to use is a time log. Get out 14 sheets of paper and date each one of them for the next 14 days. Write down everything you do from the time you wake up until the time you go to sleep. This exercise will reveal what you really believe in. It will reveal what you truly believe you must do, that you have to do, and maybe even what your flesh-driven emotions simply *want* to do!

Remember that you *value* what you do and you *do* what you value. So, your true values will be revealed through this exercise. Think about what you are doing (self-awareness) and the results you are getting, and think about how you would like that to be different. If needed, go back to the Wheel of Life and think about your life some more. Understand that values (habits) change very slowly, so be patient!

## *Step 2: Willing to Change*

Once we become aware of our habits, we must be willing to change. Remember that in order to HAVE something different, you've got to DO something different and to DO something different, you've got to BE something different. You've got to be willing to change.

Willing to change how you think. Willing to change your actions each day. Willing to make decisions that are difficult, but that will help you live the life you are really supposed to live.

Why are most people unwilling to change?

FEAR.

Fear of failure. Fear of success. Fear of the unknown. We fear that if we pursue what we really want, and we fail, we'll be a laughingstock. If we are successful we won't know how to handle it. And there are hidden fears that we can't explain (like my fear of heights), and even fears we aren't aware of. So, as you think about how you will have to change, remember the technique of overcoming fear: replace it with the truth. You may need a professional to help you through the process. And in some cases, maybe even Spiritual deliverance.

Once you are determined to face reality, you must be willing to change. In fact, you must be willing to change daily. Change is a habit that you want to create. Change the way you think about yourself. Change the way you think about the world. Change the way you think about God. Remember, the truth will set you free. You will ACT out of the belief that you have in these three areas. A man *is* as he *thinks* he is.

## The "I Can't" Factor

Speaking of that, one of the biggest reasons that goals aren't met is the "I can't" factor. When a possibility crosses your mind, you immediately discount it with "I can't do that." "That's not me." A good example is public speaking. "Oh, I could never do that," you might say to yourself. The reason? FEAR! It is said that the fear of public speaking is rated along with the fear of death! Why? Fear of failure, fear of success, and fear of the unknown.

The truth is ...

### *What one man can do,*
### *another can do!*

In a movie called *The Edge*, Anthony Hopkins and Alec Baldwin were stranded in the bitter-cold Alaskan wilderness. They were starving and were being hunted by a man-eating bear. Baldwin's character was convinced they would die. The wise character played by Hopkins had read books on survival and knew the truth – that it *is* possible to survive.

Being focused on the truth, he demanded that Baldwin repeat after him, "What one man can do, another can do!" He made him repeat it, "What one man can do, another can do!" He made him shout, "WHAT ONE MAN CAN DO, ANOTHER CAN DO!" So it is with you. What one man can do, another can do. What one woman can do, another can do.

Keeping the vision for your LIFE GOALS in mind, be willing to change to allow that to happen. Know that you are free to pursue that vision for your life. No one is holding you back. I love this quote:

*"Go confidently in the direction of your dreams. Live the life you have always imagined."* —Henry David Thoreau

Ask yourself right now how you want your life to be different. How do *you* want to be different? What do you want to *do* differently? Be as clear as you can.

Address the fear in your life. Remember that success doesn't happen in your comfort zone. Failure is required for success. But as Zig says, "Failure is an event, not a person."

The only two reasons people make drastic changes are because of inspiration or desperation. Anything in between is known as your comfort zone. There was once a mailman that walked up to an old farmer's house to deliver the mail. The farmer's hound dog was lying on the porch, moaning and howling. "What's the matter with your dog, Mister?" asked the mailman. "I think he's layin' on a nail," said the old farmer. "How come he doesn't get up?" wondered the mailman. "I guess because it don't hurt enough yet!" replied the farmer.

Until we become desperate enough to change, we won't. The problem with desperation is that once we get comfortable, we'll return to our bad habits. So, staying inspired is the key. A little self-imposed desperation is good sometimes to get yourself kick-started! Remind yourself constantly that if God is calling you to something that He will help you do it! That is the truth.

What is the COST of staying the same? What is the COST of not realizing your dreams and goals? What will you, your family, and the world miss out on by you not pursuing your dream?

This can give you the desperation you need to face your fear and begin to change.

## *Think and Grow Rich*

The steps outlined in Napoleon Hill's book distilled into a simple process are

1. Have a Burning Desire (inspiration)

2. Make a Decision (based on the TRUTH that if you are called to do it, you can)

3. Create a Definite Plan (see the 7 Steps of Implementation)

4. Assemble a Mastermind (you need support to stay focused, encouraged and accountable; you need a Dream Team.)

Will you DECIDE to change today? Who will help you through that process?

Most of what humans do comes from hidden values that we don't consciously recognize. We make excuses. So, we have to DECIDE what we want and why we want it. We make a LOGICAL decision based on FACTS, or a HUNCH, or the Holy Spirit. Then we make a decision to move in that direction. I can tell you that so many of my successes in life came as a result of making one simple decision. A moment of inspiration and decision can change your entire future.

If you haven't truly made a decision to change and do things differently, you will NOT move forward. You may be aware of your actions, but you won't get any better results unless you are willing to change. Sometimes you have to make decisions in your life based on the facts you have, even if your emotions aren't going along with it.

Our emotions have created grooves in our brains that are automatic, it takes a lot of focus to begin to change. Without being willing to change, we will immediately revert back to our usual habits because that's what we know.

## Step 3: Controlled Attention

Once you've made the decision to change, you will now begin to control attention to your new way of doing things. For example, when I first got healthy and lost 50 pounds (more on that in the next chapter), I had a great routine. My eating plan was borderline militant and my exercise was consistent. But I got bored with my exercise and I fired my trainer. I fooled myself into thinking I would stay consistent. I didn't, and because my legs weren't as strong as I thought they were, I blew out my knee playing basketball and had to have surgery. Once that happened, my eating habits changed. Result? Weight gain and a lower energy level.

That's how this phase of controlled attention works. When you first make the decision, maybe you're really inspired, but as time goes on things happen. Circumstances begin to get in the way. You've got to keep the vision alive. I lost my vision of being phenomenally fit. Fortunately, I got it back. My knee is healed and I am consistently training and playing basketball. And my eating habits have improved again.

Getting through the controlled attention phase is critical because this is where habits begin to change. If you stay the course through this phase, you have a real chance of living the phenomenal life you are called to live. Keep in mind there is also a God factor here, too. God can do things in your life that are supernatural that cannot be explained. But even when you have faith, you've got to work through the strongholds with God's help.

To get through the "controlled attention" phase, confess the truth and visualize what you want. Create a vision board that inspires you. Post your goals. Remember, your mind takes pictures. You will live out the picture that is in your mind. Whatever you set your mind on will materialize in your life.

Check every thought that comes into your mind. Take every thought captive to the obedience of Christ. Imagine that you are the gate agent on an airplane and your thoughts are passengers that want to board. Negative, destructive, ungodly thoughts cannot board because they don't have a ticket. Dismiss them and set your mind on the things that you are called to do, the things that are good for your life. The things that inspire you.

Control your thoughts. Accept or reject the thought. One of the ways to recondition your mind is to reprogram your subconscious mind. The way to do that is to focus on who you are, what the truth actually is and what your vision is. Recite it to yourself over and over when you get up and when you go to bed.

Some suggest doing this 50 times at night and 50 times in the morning. If that's what it takes for you, do it. If it takes listening to the Word of God throughout the night with ear buds, do it! For me, I have built a habit of simply lifting up my thoughts to God as soon as my feet hit the floor. I thank Him for Who He is and what He has done for me. Even if there are problems, I try to be grateful for what I have and the possibilities that are ahead. As I trained myself to do this, I would literally raise my hands to the sky and thank God as I walked through my home in the morning.

Develop a habit of writing your vision out on paper. List your goals and dreams. Visualize and write how you want to be different as a person. Create a vision board. A few years ago, I went to Michael Gerber's Dreaming Room. You get an artist's pad and Michael encourages you to use a *beginner's mind and a blank piece of paper*. With a handful of colored markers, you paint a picture of your life. Continue to visualize the picture of the life of your preferred future. Do this daily.

## Step 4: Commitment

Commitment is the stage when you become more consistent. How do you know if you have actually entered this stage? If you find yourself still waffling, you haven't truly made the decision you need to make. Stop and ask yourself why. What is the fear? What is behind the fear?

Get with your coach and review. Remember, this is a process and it comes over time. By the way, remember that all of this is in context of your goals. I hope I have made that clear by now! If you do not have clearly-defined goals, you will never know where you are going and if and when you ever get there.

If you do not have clearly-defined goals, you will be forced to focus on activity and ultimately become enslaved by it. Action without vision is a nightmare.

So, this becomes even more powerful. When we become AWARE of our ACTIONS (or inaction) that are keeping us from our goals, and we identify WHAT we need to do to get there, we have more energy to stay focused on the activity that will get us to our goal. Not just the activity, but in the context of the goal.

Goals first. Strategies second.

What if you don't have goals? You do - and I'll prove it: Do you have a favorite TV show? Or a sports team that you watch? Or a regular meeting you attend? That's a goal. It's a goal that you put on your calendar (even if it was your mind's calendar) and you were there. You just have to discover new goals. But you DO have goals. Everyone does.

You may not have discovered your life work, but you definitely have an idea of what LIFESTYLE you want to lead. You definitely have an idea of how much bottom line money you need at the end of the day.

And while I am on that subject...you must TRACK!!!!!!!!

If you don't know where you are, how can you get where you are going?

Measure everything. It's hard to improve it if you don't measure it. I got a phone call from one of my members once who said, "It's kind of slow." He wasn't tracking his numbers. When I made him do that, we discovered that he had made $30,000.00 more *that* year than he had the *previous* year!

You see, if you aren't tracking, and you are just going by feeling, then you are focusing on the wrong thing.

Back to commitment.

Once you come to the decision of what needs to be done, you begin to focus on it, and do it over and over and over, even when you don't feel like it.

EVEN WHEN YOU DON'T FEEL LIKE IT!!!

For example, as I mentioned earlier, I hated numbers. But when I connected my income statement to my dream I said to myself, "I'm going to look at these numbers until I go *snow blind* if I have to." It was hard, but I developed a system for reporting and I review my numbers on a regular basis. This is called commitment. Once you force yourself to come to this stage and you stay committed and consistent, something amazing happens...

## *Step 5: Character*

Here's where you enter the final phase. What do I mean by *character*? Someone once said that character is what you do when no one is looking. Your character is who you really are. You are what you value, you do what you value, and you value what you do. Character is the true picture of your values. It is the true test of whether an idea or desire has become a habit or not. You can test your character simply by what you actually do and don't do. Not what you *wish* you did, not what you *want* to do. Not what you *thought* about doing (or did in the past). But by what you are doing right now.

Do you finally see how this works? It's who you are that determines what you do, which determines what you have.

We do what we value and we value what we do. If you are not consistently doing it without thinking about it yet, you are not there. Press on. Continue to focus and do it over and over, even if it feels awkward. Eventually, by remaining committed, the character will come on its own. After I learned the value of reviewing my financials years ago, it became a habit.

Now I do it consistently with ease and without even thinking about it.

That's how you know it is now a true value. It's part of your character. This step comes automatically only after you have worked through the other four steps. If you stay committed, this will happen automatically. It reminds me of something I have heard. Perhaps you have, too...

## *The Four Levels of Competence*

1. Unconscious Incompetence – You are not self-aware. You don't even realize what you are doing.

2. Conscious Incompetence – You finally "see" that you are doing it all wrong. (Self-awareness)

3. Conscious Competence – As you build your new habits and skills and go through the controlled attention and commitment stages, you are conscious of your progress.

4. Unconscious Competence – This is when you know that you have built a new habit. You do it automatically. It is a way of thinking. You now have new values.

So, your character has changed. Whatever the subject matter is, when your habits have taken hold, this is what you value, which describes your true character.

So, if you aren't consistently experiencing the habits that you desire and therefore not getting the results that you want, then you need to go back through the process.

Ask yourself these questions:

1. Have I set clearly-defined goals? If not, get with your coach.

2. Am I excited and passionate? If not, take hold of the truth of being a phenomenally successful person and understand the LIFE principle, Living In Freedom Everyday™. Understand that the truth is that *what one man can do, another can do!*

3. Am I staying committed to being organized? Am I using the time capsule? Am I taking time to plan every day? Am I keeping my goals and priorities in front of me? Am I tracking where I am right now? Am I ignoring the urge to work on something that I know won't bring me the results that I need?

4. Am I implementing the very best strategies? Or am I doing them half way? Do I really understand how to do it?

5. Am I staying plugged in to my support system – my mastermind – my coach – so that others can "see" me from the outside in? Everyone needs a coach. Everyone needs others speaking into their lives.

6. Am I self-aware?

7. Am I willing to change? Have I made the decision?

8. Am I using controlled attention? Positive affirmations? Killing negative self-talk? Choosing to focus on the possibilities rather than the problems?

9. Am I forcing myself to be committed, so that my habits will change?

If so, press on, and the habits will form if you stay with it long enough. The good news is that whatever you are trying to implement in your life will most likely remain for a lifetime if you go through this process. Then you will find new levels, new areas that you want to work on, and the process starts over again.

Don't be overwhelmed. Keep the faith. Press on!

## *Shower Thinking*

In closing this chapter, let me share a very powerful thinking strategy with you. Whether you are creating the vision for your life, trying to come up with ideas, or simply trying to solve a problem, I believe this strategy will help you.

This thinking strategy is called *Free Association.* Free association is when you allow your mind to associate ideas without forcing it to do so. Your subconscious is very powerful and is always at work.

Have you ever noticed that your best ideas come to you while in the shower? Why is that? It's because your mind is relaxed. You can recreate the "shower environment" by getting in a peaceful, relaxing place. For me, it's on a beach or on a mountain, or at home, simply sitting out by the pool.

Once in a creative environment, simply start thinking about your subject. Write down every crazy thing that comes to mind. Just let your mind wander and write down what comes to mind. For example, let's say you are trying to think of a marketing strategy for your business.

Start with how much money you need to generate. Now simply write down every crazy idea that comes to your mind. Each idea will lead to another and another. I use this process to think through all of my seminars, books, dreams and goals. To be phenomenally successful you've got to take time out to think. Make it a habit to get out of the pressure cooker on a regular basis to think.

Just about every single day, I take about 30 minutes by the pool to think and plan. When I'm at the beach, it's several hours. Make creative and strategic *thinking* a **habit.**

Create a vision board with images that inspire you. Write out your perfect day. Where will you be? Who will you be with? Fill each hour of the day with exactly the life you want to live and that will bless others.

# 3

# How to Make Phenomenal Money

A couple of years ago, I began mentoring an "at-risk" kid at an elementary school through a program called Kid's Hope. My mentee began attending our church, and one Sunday afternoon, he and his grandma came to our house for a swim in the pool.

My wife and I are blessed to live in a very nice, very large custom home. As we were swimming in the pool, he blurts out, "I didn't know you were rich!" It caught me by surprise and I felt a little embarrassed and uneasy. Not knowing exactly what to say, I responded with "rich is relative," and after thinking about it, I think that's true. The fact is that compared to some people in the world, *he's* rich!

Bringing up the subject of money triggers all sorts of weird emotions. Everyone seems to want more of it, but can't stand those who have it! Like me, you may have felt a little uneasy when I shared the story about my mentee. Most people feel that they "need" more money, but aren't good with it once they get it. As our "cash flow" increases, we just get more "stuff." A television commercial from a few years ago said it best...

The spot opens with a happy guy with a grin so big he could eat a banana sideways! He brags about his big yard, his big house, his new car, and even his country club membership. Looking into the camera he says, "How do I do it? I'm in debt up to my eyeballs!" He confesses. Then he whispers into the camera, "I can barely pay my finance charges."

I can relate. I lived like that for a long time. I used what I call the *Elvis Presley Accounting Method...* Elvis would buy a stranger a Mercedes without giving it much thought. As the bills piled up, his stepfather, Vernon, and wife, Pricilla, complained. He said, "Don't worry, we can just get another gig!" And it was true. His manager, Colonel Tom Parker, could pick up the phone and generate a million dollars in an instant.

When I wanted something, I just bought it. It didn't matter how much it was. I had a lot of credit cards with big limits and I was good at generating revenue. Like Elvis, I figured there was no limit to the amount of money I could generate. I have been blessed to know how to do that – and I'm going to share that secret with you – but before too long the debt increased, the interest grew, and the payments began to mount.

Before I owned a business, I never really had much money to speak of. But when you learn how to generate cash in your business, and you become more confident in your ability to increase sales, you're tempted to take more risks. As our overhead grew and it became more difficult to "make the payments," we maxed out our lines of credit and started paying ridiculous credit card rates.

## Something had to give

Fortunately, for me, the Grace of God was waiting for me. I didn't have to face a financial meltdown. And my wife is good at making money AND saving it! She is amazing. In the early days, we used savings from her paycheck to make payroll. I shudder to think what my life would be like without God and my wife!

I found some really good financial consultants, and my good friend and business partner Scott Zack helped me realize that following Dave Ramsey's philosophy of being debt-free and operating from a healthy profit would serve me much better.

I'm a very generous person and kind of like Elvis, I like to give money away. I love to bless people. When I was deep in debt, I still gave as much as I could, but when your giving becomes limited to what you can put on a card, it's sad. The more interest I paid, the less I could help others. Now, understand that we were still investing in our 401k, my wife was investing faithfully, and we were tithing. So, we weren't destitute or poor. Just not enough cash flow to handle the commitments.

Then there's the whole tax issue – you've got to either pay a lot of income tax or buy stuff for the business. So we bought lots of trucks, equipment, and things like that to lower our tax burden, while at the same time trying to maximize tax deferred stuff like 401k to reduce the tax burden. I refinanced my home and commercial building and took the equity out.

I like to spend money, too. There's a LOT I want to DO and HAVE in life. I wanted to get ALL the dream NOW and my flawed thinking was to finance the dream. Get everything you need now. Pay for it later. I didn't really understand how much was going out in finance charges and how it was actually stealing my dream.

It's no way to live. There's no freedom in it. Living a phenomenally successful L.I.F.E. doesn't have room for undue stress. When your financial life is like a loose cannon rolling around on deck, you don't know what's going to get blasted next! Most divorces are caused by money problems. Many relationships are destroyed because of money issues.

So I became WILLING TO CHANGE. I began to change my thinking about money. I began to change my thinking about debt. And I can tell you that because of that, my businesses have become much more profitable and effective. There is more freedom personally. I can help more people, too.

How I value other people has served me well, even in this area of my life. No matter how hard it was, I paid everyone I owed. Little by little the debt went down and then I got phenomenally profitable. It's a great feeling.

This chapter is about making phenomenal money. The question is how much is "phenomenal"? It may be one thing to me and another to you. How much money should YOU make? You might be surprised at my answer...

You should make the amount of money that you are "supposed" to have. Remember that the financial area of your L.I.F.E. is one of the important spokes on the Wheel of Life. Your vision for your life is your calling, your purpose. So how much money is required to fulfill that vision?

When you figure out what your L.I.F.E. G.O.A.L.S.! ™ are and what you are supposed to do in life, you will know how much money you are supposed to have. I believe that's one of the reasons people don't have more money to work with. They don't know how much they're supposed to have!

Most people simply take what they get and hope that some more drops in their life. They wish they would win the lottery, get a better job, or that some miracle would happen. The hard lesson that I have learned is that first, you've got to figure out how much you need to fulfill your vision, and you've got to go get it. When you get it, you've got to keep the amount you're supposed to keep, use the amount you are supposed to use, and give the amount you're supposed to give.

## *So, let's talk about you and your money...*

In coaching hundreds of small business owners and interacting with thousands, I am amazed how many owe back taxes, their home is about to be fore-closed upon and they're hanging by a financial thread. Many of them have every kind of money problem you can imagine. They're dreading the drop of the proverbial "second shoe." "I owe, I owe, so off to work I go" is the motto. To make matters worse, they DON'T know how to make money.

So, this chapter is really about making money. How to make PHENOMENAL money. That's if you are supposed to make phenomenal money. No matter the amount of money you are supposed to have access to, whether it is large or small, I think it would be phenomenal if you hit that mark, don't you?

If you're deep in debt, start following the Dave Ramsey philosophy. There's no freedom in debt. The next step is to determine how you value money. Our values surrounding money are exactly like all of the other values we have picked up like germs off the street – often they're emotional, irrational, senseless feelings that have no basis in truth.

Every person on the planet has a money con-sciousness that has been bred over their lifetime, just like every other unchecked value. A phenomenally successful life is about checking every belief you have to determine whether it's true or not. The same goes for how you value money. T. Harv Ecker's book, *Secrets of a Millionaire Mind,* does a good job of explaining this. Robert Kiosaki's *Rich Dad, Poor Dad* series also does a good job of explaining how money works and how to make it work for you.

Now, please understand that as a person of faith, you want to trust God for everything. Much of our conflict comes from avoiding "the love of money" and when you are successful and blessed, people will accuse you of that. God will lead you to know what you are supposed to do, which will lead you to how much you are supposed to have. By the same token, you have to act on what you are supposed to do. If God is leading you to DO something and you just sit around waiting for God to do what YOU are supposed to do, it ain't gonna work. Too often, we wait around on God when He's saying "go!"

Can you keep a lot of it for retirement and go on vacation, etc.? I think so. But I'm not the one to tell you how much money is enough for you. I can only tell you that there is an amount that you are supposed to have, because there are specific things you are supposed to do in your life.

It took a lot of money to keep Gandhi poor. Jesus didn't own anything, but money was used to run the ministry. But Jesus didn't have a mortgage. If you are deep in debt and can barely pay your finance charges like the guy in the tv spot, you need to make more money or you've got to unload some stuff. I don't think owing everyone in the world because you're avoiding the "love of money" is very spiritual. That's NOT very phenomenal! So, you've got to figure out what you're supposed to do in life, so that you will know how much money you are supposed to have.

## *How to Make PHENOMENAL Money...*

Now that you understand that you need to generate money for specific purposes, the best way to make phenomenal money is to own a phenomenally successful business. Notice I didn't say "own a business" - I said a *phenomenally* successful business! As you will see in the next chapter, there IS a difference! Too many people who own businesses have become prisoners of the business AND they're broke! If you're going to go broke, at least enjoy it! Go to the beach, sit on your back porch and sip tea, but to be stressed out and work 24/7 and go broke is no way to live. It's *not* very phenomenal!

Sure, many of them love what they do and from the outside it looks glamorous, but the truth is they are miserable. But the prospect of working for someone else isn't even an option, so they just put their head down and continue on the hamster wheel.

So if you're in business, or you take my advice below to at least start a part-time business, do yourself a favor and admit what you don't know about business and be willing to change. The next chapter will help you a great deal.

Please understand that I am not saying that you can't make phenomenal money in a job. There are plenty of folks that have phenomenal jobs. If they are smart with their money, and they enjoy the overall benefits their job brings, go for it! But if you want to get yourself in a position to make money without having to work a "job," then there may be a business for you. But you must begin to think like a business owner rather than an employee.

Maybe you have a job, but you're not ready to become a full-time entrepreneur. A part-time business, or a business that you have others run for you, might be the right fit.

You may be loathing the idea of owning a business. You may be fearful of owning you own business. But remember – fear is most often not based on fact.

You may just be unaware of how to go about it. One of the things you will learn as a phenomenally successful person is not to worry about "how" as much as "what" and "why." Example: you need to increase your income by a certain amount (what), because you aren't making enough to cover your bills (why). There are many ways (the "how") to do it. Strategies and ideas are a dime a dozen, but action and courage are lacking.

So, if you have a big WHY (you want to send your kid to college, you want to make a difference in the world, or you're just tired of being broke and in debt), then a phenomenally successful business is for you.

### *Here are three suggestions for you...*

My son is going to Texas Tech University in Lubbock, Texas, this year and his soon-to-be dorm-mate joined us for a week at our condo in Florida. He expressed some interest in owning his own business, so I shared with him that I would look in three directions if I were him...

**1. A Service Business.** The first business I started is a service business. I started out of the trunk of my car. Rather than sitting at home in the evenings or on your days off, you could be generating hundreds of dollars per hour. With technology today, some leadership skill and a little business savvy, you can even get others to do the work for you. Speaking of college students, what great, smart, part-time (no benefits) employees they can be!

1-800-GOT-JUNK was started with one pick-up truck. How much investment is required to pick up junk? None. Now, the company bills *$100 million* in revenue! The company collects a 17% royalty which means it rakes in $17M in annual revenue!

**2. A Network Marketing Business.** The second type of business is a network marketing business, also known as *multi-level marketing.* This is a business that has a direct sales force that is made up of independent distributors that sell the product and recruit others to get paid.

Wait a minute...I can hear you saying, "You mean kind of like a 'pyramid scheme?'" Unfortunately, the network marketing industry is absolutely rampant with those with a lot of zeal and not much wisdom on how they approach prospects. Typically, they burn through friends and family with a lot of pressure, making people feel uncomfortable. The worst part is that those who could make a lot of money with network marketing never get the opportunity, because they ASSUME that somehow it's wrong.

Network marketing is a legitimate business model. Maybe one of the most ingenious models ever created. Why? Because you can get started with a cell phone and an Internet connection (something that many 10-year-olds have today!) and a few dollars and you're in business. You don't need employees, equipment or a building. You can live wherever you want and work around a job, baby-sitting, school or whatever occupies your time.

### *What you need to be successful...*

Regardless of the type of business you start, you need customers and you need a product or service. If you are not willing to learn how to find customers and understand how to communicate the benefits of a service or product, you aren't going to be successful. Go back and think about your dreams, goals and vision from Chapter 1. If making more money could help you reach that, wouldn't it be worth getting out of your comfort zone to learn how to build a business? When I started my first business at age 23, I knew nothing about running a business. I had a heart to serve and to be the best. Do you? That's all you need.

You can learn the rest. In fact, in the next chapter, you will get some insights. The next chapter is mainly written for those who already have a business. I hope it doesn't scare you off, because most small business owners become slaves to their businesses. But you can avoid that altogether.

My favorite network marketing business is Send Out Cards. www.SendOutCards.com. Send Out Cards is a greeting card business that allows you to choose a greeting card online and they PRINT IT and MAIL IT through the U.S. mail in a plain white envelope. It looks handwritten, but you don't have to stuff and mail it yourself. Everyone seems to agree that sending thank you cards, anniversary, birthday and Christmas cards is important, but few actually implement.

This is especially important for business owners and sales professionals. There are a few things that really set Send Out Cards apart that you can't get with any other service.

*The biggest benefit*
*is you can make money*
*while making a difference!*

Here are the benefits of Send Out Cards...

1. Choose from over 16,000 greeting cards.

2. This is NOT an online card. <u>They send it through the mail!</u>

3. You can use hand-written fonts.

4. You can even upload your own handwriting!

5. Upload your signature as well as three other signatures (you and your spouse, your family or company signature).

6. Upload pictures from your computer into the card!!!

7. Create your own card from any picture on your computer with ease.

8. Automatic reminder for birthdays and anniversaries.

9. Mail ONE card to AS MANY PEOPLE YOU WANT! Each card is personalized!

10. It's easy to upload your contact list.

11. Create groups so you can send cards to specific groups.

12. Create multi-card, sequential cards. Example, let's say you have a "New Client" Campaign. That campaign educates your clients, patients, members or volunteers.

13. Send gifts along with the cards: Gift cards such as Starbucks, Home Depot, etc., chocolates, cookies and Send Out Card's famous brownies, as well as many gourmet foods, books and audio CDs, gifts for the home, men, women, etc.

One of the things you will learn about me is that I am recognized world-wide as an expert on something called "relationship marketing." All of business and all of life really is about relationships. Building positive relationships starts with caring and caring starts with giving. Personalized, meaningful greeting cards and gifts are a phenomenal way to do that. I call Send Out Cards *the greatest marketing tool of all time* because of what it can do.

In 2009 I personally sponsored more people than the 25,000 distributors Send Out Cards had at the time. I know how to sell and I made a *significant* amount of money with Send Out Cards. I still get nice checks just about every week.

### *I didn't make as much as I could have – and not nearly as much as you can...*

I could have made a LOT more money with Send Out Cards. Why? Because I didn't build a team. Those who are making millions of dollars per year in network marketing do it by building a team. That may sound scary, but it's not that hard. My intention is to still build a team with Send Out Cards, so you can be on my team and we'll work together.

## *When you join Send Out Cards, you will need a Sponsor ID.*

## *My ID is 7162*

At this moment, as you are evaluating this idea, you may be tempted to immediately dismiss it because you have no basis of fact. **The habit of dismissing something totally on emotion is one that you will want to overcome to become a phenomenally successful person.** Get the facts first. Seek to understand – then make your judgment. I used to think the same thing, by the way. Now I know that people are making fortunes in network marketing.

**3. Information Marketing.** The third suggestion is to start a business in the *Information Marketing* field. People are looking for all types of information online – *how to start a business* – *how to learn to play piano* or *how to train a dog*. Once you learn how to capture the people who are searching the terms, you can then offer them a product or service they are looking for.

The best part is that you don't even have to create the information yourself unless you want to. There are plenty of experts on the subject of choice that already have the product or service that are more than willing to pay you when you refer someone. You don't have to be the expert! Think about Oprah. What is she an expert at? Nothing that comes to mind. But she is an expert at *finding experts* and generating an audience.

### *Don't worry, you don't have to be the next Oprah!*

You can start out very small. You can put up a nice little blog and open a PayPal account and you're ready to make money. Find something you are really passionate about. Search some terms on the Internet and when you find someone who has a great product, service or valuable information for sale, contact them to see if they will pay you a commission. Now, all you have to do is learn how to get traffic, and that's a skill that can be learned.

You may wonder why I recommend starting a business instead of just working harder or longer. If you have the opportunity to take a second job, or earn more money working, by all means do it. But you are trading labor for dollars and that's not how you make phenomenal money. If you are supposed to have phenomenal money, you may or may not be able to generate it working a job.

If you already have a business that's not phenomenally successful, we'll see if we can help you fix that. I'll get into the strategies of building a phenomenal business in the next chapter, but this chapter is about money. Phenomenal money. Once you know how much you are supposed to have, you've got to understand HOW to get it.

### *The ONE and ONLY reason your business exists is to help you achieve your L.I.F.E Goals!*

Period. End of story. There is no other reason it exists. Would you agree that your business has a dramatic impact on your personal life? And if it actually *destroys* your life, what good is it?

The everyday demands of a business have a dramatic impact on our personal lives. The good news (no, *phenomenal* news) is that it can be POSITIVE! It doesn't have to be negative. So, the first step toward a phenomenal business is to understand *why* it exists – to enhance your life and deliver on the life goals that you may not be able to realize with a regular *job*.

You must get the fact that your business works for you. You don't work for the business. Your business is a *vehicle* to help you live out your life goals. It's *the* vehicle you have chosen.

Don't get me wrong – you'll still work just as hard – and if you don't have money, you may have to invest more "sweat equity" than you ever imagined to get it where you need it to be. You may have to work long and hard in the beginning. But if you design your life goals *first* and build your business around that, you will avoid much of the heartache that comes with "action without vision."

I often ask my seminar attendees how big they want to get. Oftentimes the answer is "as big as possible." Although I admire the confidence and enthusiasm, building the business just for the sake of "getting bigger" with no real vision of *why* you are doing it and how it will affect you personally, will likely result in the owner being a slave to the business. And the other "spokes" on the Wheel of Life will suffer.

When I first read *The E-Myth Revisited*, I finally understood how to stop being a slave to my business. Michael Gerber talks about your *primary aim*. When you design a compelling, purposeful, phenomenal picture for your life and design your business around your life goals, you'll approach your business with more purpose and direction.

You will have a compelling *reason* to build it. With a compelling vision for your life, you'll be willing to learn what you need to learn and, more important, implement it.

The other side of the proverbial coin is that your personal habits have a dramatic impact on your business. To grow a phenomenal business, you've got to become a phenomenally successful person with positive habits. Just knowing how to build a business is not enough.

So, once you realize that your business exists to help you achieve your Life Goals, you design your life first. Then you work "on" the business to design it to fulfill that ideal picture. Now you have a compelling reason to work on your business. You will be willing to learn what you need to learn. Otherwise, just gaining knowledge about building your business will be useless. You might use a little bit of it to do "better," but it's not about being "better." It's about living out the calling, the vision that you have for your life.

I was having lunch with a very successful business owner friend of mine who feels like he is at a crossroads. The business he really loves and feels connected to isn't set up to really help him reach his dreams in life. He has a condition that could take his life. His dream is to make sure his family doesn't have to struggle should that occur.

His other business, that is doing very well and could help him reach all of his dreams in life, is not getting the attention it needs. He's conflicted (like we all get sometimes).

I shared the story about the monkey and the banana with him. A monkey found a banana in a jar.

He had his hand on the banana, but couldn't get it through the small mouth of the jar. At the same time, there was another banana just out of reach on the ground (that he could very easily reach). But he wouldn't let go of the banana in the jar.

I could see tears welling up in my friend's eyes as I shared the banana story.

The banana in the jar represents the business that he has to continually re-invent that won't get him his ultimate dream. The banana on the ground represents the business that will help him reach his dream. Getting completely focused on his true life goal of providing for his family's future, rather than the immediate dollars he can make now, will help him take the action he needs to take in his other business.

## The #1 Reason Most Small Businesses Don't Grow (or do as well as they could)

A few years ago, I was sharing the "Vision without action is a daydream" proverb during a keynote presentation, and my friend Kirby Lammers chuckled and muttered "F.T.I." I asked him what it meant. He said a speaker he heard once called it "Failure To Implement." Many times you know *what* to do and *how* to do it, you just *don't* do it. After coaching hundreds of business owners and addressing thousands, I have found that F.T.I. is the NUMBER ONE problem. The question is *why*?

No compelling vision for your life. No real hope of ever reaching your dream. Have you noticed that the most successful small business owners are enthusiastic? Have you noticed they are *excited*?

They see something others don't see. They have hope for the future because they *know* they can grow the business. They *know* they can improve their lives.

### *Inspiration to Implementation*

I call that *inspiration*. Too many times we have distractions, a lack of focus and a lack of discipline. Business owners aren't organized or motivated. The reason? They aren't inspired. Why aren't they inspired? They don't have a compelling, meaningful vision that drives them every day. You MUST get that!

This is my hope for you – that you get a new, inspiring vision as a result of reading this book. If you've owned your own business for a while, you probably realize that what I am saying is true. In this chapter I will share the secrets of a phenomenal business – instead of hitting roadblocks, I'm going to show you the roadmap to a predictable, profitable, TURNKEY operation.

## *Are you ready?*

A turnkey business is one that is systematized to the point that the owner doesn't have to be involved in the day-to-day operations of the business. Most people think it's a fantasy, but I've proven it is not. And I've helped others do it. They are experiencing so much more freedom in their businesses and lives.

It doesn't mean you won't have problems. It doesn't mean you won't have to do anything – and it doesn't mean that you don't have responsibilities. It also doesn't mean that you can just escape without first creating the infrastructure you need. It *does* mean that if you will take the time to learn and implement the secrets (the things most people don't know), you will be in a position to make it a reality.

Most small business owners are convinced that no one can do the technical part of the business as good as they can. And that's the very reason you are a slave to your business! You may have hired nightmare employees in the past and now you're gun-shy. If you're a solo entrepreneur, you may be convinced that you need to stay that way, but does that truly fit with your life goals? If you have a large business and your employees are running you, I have hope for you, too.

### *How to put your business on auto-pilot with S.Y.S.T.E.M.S.*

If you want to have a predictable, profitable turn-key operation – or you just want things to run more smoothly, you've got to have systems. My systems acronym stands for:

**S**ystematizing

**Y**our

**S**trategies

**T**o

**E**xecute

**M**anagement

**S**uccessfully

Everyone has strategies. You may not realize how many strategies you have, but you have specific ways that you do things. You may have intentionally decided to answer your phone a certain way rather than another, for example. That's a *strategy*. There's a certain way you do your work.

That's a *strategy.* There's a certain way you advertise. That's a *strategy.*

A system is a group of working parts that are *designed* to work *together.* Then and only then can you really execute successfully. Then and only then can you really *manage.*

By the way, even if you are a solo operator or an independent professional that works alone, you need systems. There is a specific order of things that works best. If you do it the same way each time, you increase your results. If you get off of the procedure, you risk not getting the same results. Once you have tested a number of strategies, you find what works best and duplicate it over and over.

## *Why systems are critical to your business*

Systems are the key to profitable growth. The bigger you get without systems, the more money is going out the door in re-inventing every day. Employees perform better because they aren't micro-managed and they know exactly what they are supposed to accomplish. You have fewer surprises because they aren't trying to make it up every time.

It also keeps you, the owner, in line. If you are like me, you like to tinker with it and change things around. If you have a team, they're confused. Then the customer is confused. When you change something, be sure to communicate it and update the *system*.

This is probably one of the biggest reasons for systems – your client, patient, member or guest. They get a consistent service experience. When it is done the same way every time, the customer has confidence in what to expect.

Finally, would you like to sell your business one of these days? Let's face facts. Anyone with a significant amount of money to invest doesn't want your 24-hour-a-day-7-day-a-week job! How much is your job worth?

Anyone interested in buying a business wants to buy a turnkey operation. An investor simply wants a set of keys. He invests his money and turns the key to start his new money machine. That's all he wants. If it revolves around your controlling and directing every facet of the business, it is of no use to him as an investor.

## *The 5 Vital Components of a System*

I believe if you understand the following components that you can systematize just about anything.

Assembling these five components creates the ulti-mate system. I believe these will work for any type of business or organization

**The 5 Components are...**

1. **The Mission**

2. **The Organizational Chart**

3. **Job Description**

4. **Policies**

5. **Procedures**

## *Component # 1:*
## *The Mission*

The mission is what you are trying to accomplish every single day. In other words, what are you deliv-ering? For example the mission of my service com-pany is *To Provide the Most Outstanding Service Experience Ever!*

The Starbucks Mission Statement is *to establish Starbucks as the premier purveyor of the finest coffee in the world while maintaining our uncompromising principles as we grow.*

A mission is not some long, mysterious, boring paragraph hanging in the lobby of a company that no one actually knows (or believes). In fact, I recommend one sentence.

Once you have a mission that you believe in, you can use it to make every decision in your business. What kind of equipment should we use? (In the book *Onward*, Howard Shultz shares how the coffee makers that were chosen to boost profits actually killed their mission.) What kind of marketing should we do? What should our uniforms look like?

You can be tempted to do things that keep you from accomplishing your mission because you are trying to save money or you're growing so fast that you lose sight of what got you there. That's what happened to Starbucks.

In the book *Onward – How Starbucks Fought for Its Life without Losing Its Soul*, Howard Shultz shares how they regained their brand after losing their way. It's a powerful story about the importance of mission and brand.

When you have a mission that is understood, you can "check" every decision that is made.

A clear mission helps you "rally the troops" and gives you a context for coaching. When an employee doesn't follow procedure, you can simply tie the correct behavior to the "why" behind the procedure – which is the mission. Instead of your employee just thinking that you're mad at them or you don't like them or whatever emotional issue they have, they understand that it's about the mission.

They understand that the mission is best for the client. Speaking of clients, be sure to communicate your mission to your prospects, customers and clients, as well. At our company, our UEP™ (Unique Experience Proposition) is our Mission Statement. This is what the client is buying and this is what my staff provides.

What a thing of beauty!

The Ritz-Carlton does a phenomenal job with this. They have a credo card that each one of their "Ladies and Gentlemen" carries. It has their credo, motto, and three steps of service on it. Read all about it in my friend Joseph Michelli's book, *The New Gold Standard.*

The reason the mission is the very first component in building systems is we must know what it is that we are trying to accomplish each day. While you are getting your procedures in place, your team needs to know what the mission is so that they can make the right decisions. You also need your mission in place so that you can create the right procedures.

By the way, you may have heard people use the words "vision" and "mission" interchangeably. The difference between vision and mission, by the way (in my mind's eye), is this:

Mission is what your business is trying to DO each day. In other words, every time we pick up the phone, it communicates "the most outstanding service experience ever" – or it doesn't. Simple as that.

Vision is what you want your business to LOOK like. In other words, your vision is what you get when you reach your goals. We want to do X number of dollars in business, X number of clients, X dollars in profit, etc. We want to have X number of trucks, staff, etc.

Finally, your mission is supported by your VALUES or what Starbucks calls "guiding principles." These values help us live out our mission each day. My company has five values that we live by and that we communicate to our clients.

If we live out the values, we accomplish the mission. Simple as that.

To create your own mission statement, think about what you want the client to get. What do you want them to *feel*? Put together a simple but meaningful sentence and begin to communicate it to your staff. Post it on your materials, your walls, and every place it can be visible to remind you, your staff, and your clients what you are actually selling.

## *Component #2:*
## *The Organizational Chart*

Owning your own business can be overwhelming because of the number of "hats" you have to wear. Someone not only has to do the "technical" work of the business, but someone has to market, someone has to go on sales calls, someone has to do the book-keeping, someone has to order supplies, someone has to fix the equipment, and the list goes on.

If you are a larger company and you have peo-ple actually doing some of these things, you are most likely overwhelmed as you try to "manage" them and end up being involved in many things that you don't want to be involved in (and probably shouldn't be).

You are involved in too many areas because you haven't learned the skill of leadership and systems. How do you ever get over this? You need a vision. A road map – a clear picture of the business. A great tool is an Organizational Chart.

## *The Organizational Chart of most companies looks like this...*

| FUNCTION | MARKETING | SALES | OPERATIONS | ADMINISTRATION |
|---|---|---|---|---|
| Director | You | You | You | You |
| Manager | You | You | You | You |
| Technician | You | You | You | You |

No wonder you're overwhelmed! You're in every box!

So, how do you get organized? You begin by understanding the 12 vital functions of the business. Every one of these functions is vital to be phenomenally successful in your business. And if you want a turnkey business, all of them are absolutely crucial.

Does someone have to plan the business to be more successful? You bet. That's the role of what I call the "Director." Does someone have to manage the business? Absolutely. Someone must make sure that all of the things that are supposed to happen actually get implemented. I call that the "Manager."

And, of course, someone has to actually do the work of the business. The good news is that it doesn't always have to be you. And men, your wife is not the only one that can answer the phone and do the books. She needs a life, too.

So, understanding the three levels (Director, Manager and Technician) gives you a picture of how to separate and organize the major functions.

Then there are what I call the Four Pillars of a Phenomenally Successful Business. You can read about those later in this chapter.

## *How to Use the Organizational Chart*

Begin to replace yourself in the bottom boxes. Start with the things that aren't getting done and the things you despise doing (I know there are some of those!). Start with the things you aren't good at.

I started my first company out of the trunk of my car. My name was in every box. Of course, at that time I didn't even know there *were* boxes! Eventually I hired an assistant. Then I hired a couple of technicians. Then I hired people to answer the phone. Then I merged with a couple of other small business owners and put one in charge of operations and the other in charge of administration.

We then hired people to do inside sales and on-location sales. Eventually, I got someone doing marketing with me and then for me. Finally, I was only in two boxes – "Marketing Director" and "Sales Director."

Today my business is turnkey. Although I meet with my staff once a week and we work on projects, I don't really have a "job" in that business other than the responsibility of owning the business.

Systematizing your business can be done. A turn-key business *is* possible. But you must have a compelling vision to drive you. Without it, you will never do the hard work (yes, the hard work) of building systems in your business.

I knew I wanted to do what I am doing now. My vision to do that drove me to build a turnkey business. You can do it, too.

## *The Four Roles of the Business Owner*

On the Wheel of Life, there's a spoke called "Career." You want to think about what *role* you want to fulfill in your small business. Don't worry about *how* right now. Just think about your life goals and what kind of work lifestyle you are after. Remember that you want to design your business around your life goals. There are four roles you can choose to fulfill in your small business

1. **The Technician.** What I mean by "technician" is the one doing the "technical" work of the business. In a service business, the technician role is obvious, but even if you run a retail store, or you are an independent professional, the doing of the work is what I am talking about – making the sales call, processing paperwork or serving a customer. It is the *doing* of the work. Is there anything wrong with being the technician in your business?

   Absolutely NOT! If that's what you truly love to do – if that's what you are called to do - and you can balance your life, it may be a wonderful thing for you. You may want to do what doctors do – get an administrative staff and a number of assistants around you so that you can grow your "practice." All of the concepts in this chapter will assist you, even if you want to continue doing the technical work. But you must organize the other aspects of the business so you are not so overwhelmed. I want you to be the "technician" because you *want* to, not because you feel you *have* to!

2. **The Customer Service Manager.** This level is when you have others doing the

majority of the technical work, but you are still managing the service experience. A good example of this is an in-home service company. Say you are a plumber and you are normally the one that does the work. Once you develop a system, even an ordinary plumber can get extraordinary results by simply using the system that you have developed. You are still "controlling" the client experience by directing the action. You talk to the client over the phone and sometimes stop in on jobs.

3. **The General Manager.** At this level, you have a team that does most of the day-to-day duties – marketing, sales, service, and accounting. But you are there to direct the operation. Sure, you can take a vacation and leave someone in charge, but you call the day-to-day shots.

4. **The Turnkey Business Owner.** This is a level that I think all business owners dream of, but, sadly, few ever reach. You have management in place that call the day-to-day shots. You can do what you want to do, when you want to do it. If you want to go away for the summer, you can. Some people believe this is a fantasy. Of course,

I'm living proof that this can be done and I've helped others do it, too.

But let's look at some examples that maybe you can relate to...Walmart and Sam's. Could Sam Walton be in every store? No. He loved to be involved where he could, but it was impossible for him to be involved in everything that happened at Sam's and Walmart. "But Howard, that's a HUGE company. What does that have to do with me?" you might ask.

### *At one time,*
### *Sam Walton had ONE store!*

What about Warren Buffet? Does he answer the phone at Geico and write insurance? No. Does he work the floor at the Omaha-based furniture store that he owns? Of course not. So, the point here is that you have to start somewhere. And the place you want to start is getting your business systematized and organized so it is more predictable. You want to begin the process of replacing yourself in the areas that you are not good at and that you are not supposed to do.

Keeping in mind that you are supposed to make the amount of money that you are supposed to make as we learned in Chapter 2, let's think about the "Financial" spoke on the Wheel of Life.

As a business owner, your business is probably your only source of income. I was watching ABC's *Shark Tank* last night (a show that features a panel of investors and entrepreneurs seeking capital). This guy's business had done only $53,000 in sales and he was doing all the work. One of the "sharks" asked, "How do you make money?"

"My wife works," he responded.

That was the reality for me for a while! (Thank you, Denise, and my dad and everyone else who helped me when I was first starting out.)

The "Financial" spoke on the Wheel of Life represents your personal income that is taken from the business. The **NET INCOME** of your business is what contributes to your "Financial" spoke. Now that you have determined what role you want to fulfill in your business, and what your lifestyle should look like, you now want to determine how much money you want to make from the business.

Here's a simple outline of *every* income statement for *every* business. It doesn't matter whether your business is a part-time, home-based business or one of Warren Buffet's companies, *every* company has the *same* income statement.

Income

-Cost of Goods Sold (COGS)

=GP (Gross Profit)

-Fixed Expense

=Net

Income is all revenue brought in by the business. Cost of goods sold is the expenses that are directly related to producing the product or service, materials, labor, etc. Fixed expenses are those that stay relatively the same regardless of big swings in revenue. This would be rent, salaries, etc. Although there may be things that vary, they aren't tied to production.

Time and space in this book doesn't allow me to make all of the points needed to answer every question about this subject, and there is much understanding needed in the financial area. In addition to your income statement, you will want to understand your balance sheet and many other financial factors in your business. Contact Phenomenal Products for more information on this important area of your business.

For now, make a decision about how much NET INCOME you need to fulfill your Life Goals. This is where you want to start. Write down how much you need to make *annually*. Don't worry about how yet, just write it down. Remember, you'll have to pay tax on that, so figure that out as well.

Once you determine how much NET IN-COME you need, the next step is to determine your cost of doing business and determine what your BUSINESS INCOME needs to be. This is your SALES GOAL. If you don't have a 12-month financial forecast (a.k.a. "budget") for your business, you're driving blind and committing "action without vision."

If you have already resolved this issue in your business and see what we are talking about as elementary, move on. There will be some phenomenal stuff for you, too...

### *The Phenomenal Profits 747 Business Model*

The Boeing 747 jet is a humongous jet that can take a LOT of people a LONG way! And that's what you want your business to do. Please understand that like a 747, your business can be a phenomenal vehicle to help a lot of people.

Your small business can have more influence than any other man-made institution in America. If your business is truly a functioning, productive, positive *community,* you can have a phenomenal impact on many lives.

Everyone has a longing for belonging. I believe we are created with not only a "God-shaped void," but also a "people-shaped void." We were created to belong to one another. People want so desperately to be accepted, loved and belong, yet we have given up on government and many feel that religion has failed them. (Note: I am not talking about the Spiritual church, but man-made religion.)

Your business can fill that longing for belonging. You can help people grow and reach their potential. You can have incredible influence to help others live phenomenal lives.

That's the exciting part. You can not only live a phenomenal life yourself, but you can help your family, fellow faith members, employees, clients, vendors, and everyone you touch in your community, tap into the phenomenon, too.

After all, it's *not* just about you. Right?

So the first 7 in 747 stands for the 7 Spokes on the Wheel of Life that I shared in Chapter One.

### *The "4" stands*
### *for the Four Pillars of a*
### *Phenomenal Business*

There are four major pillars of every business that must be as strong as possible to be phenomenally successful. Of course, there are many sub-parts, but these major areas I call "pillars" are the first step to looking at your business as a whole.

Once you understand the pillars and their function, just like supporting a building, you can begin to strengthen the ones that are weak, therefore increasing the value and function of that building.

## Pillar #1:
## MARKETING

Marketing is everything you do to attract *prospects* to your business. Until then, they are just a *suspect*. This includes advertising, referral programs, client mailers, Internet marketing, networking, direct selling, and any other things you might do to attract prospects to your business.

Do you have enough sales? Are you getting the type of client you want? Have you even thought about your perfect target market? Are you generating enough referrals? Are you spending too much on advertising? Unless you are truly in complete demand and booked up as much as you want, then there is work to do in this area.

## *Phenomenal Marketing*

What comes to your mind when you think of marketing? For some, the first thing that comes to mind is advertising. Others think of face-to-face sales or networking. Still others think of "getting your name out there," or branding.

The function of marketing, whether it is advertising or promoting your business at the local Chamber of Commerce, has one function and one function only, and that is to **increase sales**. At the end of the day, your marketing must increase sales. It obviously must bring qualified prospects that you can convert into clients. If it fails to do that, it is not working. Too many business owners spend lots of time and money "getting their name out there," but their efforts don't produce sales.

## *The ONLY Three Ways to Increase Sales*

Regardless of the type of business you are in, there are only three ways to increase sales under the sun. The three ways are...

1. Get a higher price

2. Get more clients

3. Get more sales from existing clients

**1. Get a Higher Price.** If you are able to increase your price without losing too much in volume, your top line will increase. If you raise your price 20% and lose 20% of your sales volume, you are still making more profit. If you raise your price 50% and lose 50% of your sales volume, you are still making more profit.

## *How to get a higher price for your service – and have people stand in line to pay it*

Over the years I have positioned myself at the highest price in three industries and have helped others do the same. The key to getting a higher price for your service is to *position* yourself in the right niche. We call it *getting rich in the niche*!

In the classic marketing book *Positioning,* Jack Trout and Al Ries explain that positioning is really taking up a "slot" in the mind of your target market. Kind of like a file cabinet has a specific file for a specific brand. For example, when I say *laundry detergent*, what comes to mind? When I say *soft drink*, what comes to mind? And *luxury car*? You see, there is a brand that occupies that file in your mind.

Your goal is to position your brand in the mind of your perfect niche market. Why a niche market? If you try to be everything to everyone, you won't be anything significant to anyone.

This is what Starbucks has done with coffee. It's what Harley Davidson has done with motorcycles and what Whole Foods has done in the natural foods industry. It doesn't matter what you think of these companies. What matters is that the target market for each of these companies has embraced the brand and enthusiastically hands over their money.

To learn more about positioning your company, contact Phenomenal Products. We offer training programs to help you do this.

## 2. Get More Clients.

### *Phenomenal Referral Marketing*

#### *How to get as many high end clients as you want (without expensive advertising)*

Everyone agrees that "word of mouth" is the best advertising. Everyone knows the power in someone telling another person about a service or a product. The problem is that "casual" referrals do not always create a phenomenally successful business. To generate a massive number of referrals, you need a phenomenal referral marketing system.

There are many other ways to market your business that we also use. Direct marketing and Internet marketing strategies we use are very good, but our biggest return comes from our referral marketing.

What I mean by referral marketing is *marketing to a referral source rather than directly to the end user.* This is especially important with high end clients. High end clients (we will call them Mercedes Clients in this illustration) prefer to buy through a referral. Typically, a high end client will get a referral from a trusted friend or a trusted advisor – a consultant who in turn refers you – another consultant.

### *My definition of referral marketing:*

*"The process of building a **network** of <u>sources</u> that will refer multiple clients to your business."*

## *Top 10 Reasons Referral Marketing is So Effective*

**Reason #1:** Your Network is Unlimited – As you begin to build relationships with powerful referral sources and you get your clients to refer you, the network continues to grow with no end in sight.

**Reason #2: Higher Quality Clients** – Since Mercedes Clients seek out a referral, you get higher quality clients just from being "referral based." Referred clients usually don't even ask about the price. They are more concerned about quality than price.

**Reason #3: Pre-Qualified Clients** – By educating your referral sources, your prospective clients will be pre-qualified; therefore, they will already know you charge more.

**Reason #4: People Trust Referrals** – Wouldn't you agree that referrals already have a level of trust for you? Sure they do. They trust you because the person they trust knows about you.

**Reason #5: Reduces Competition** – With referral marketing, you are no longer fighting for the best ad placement, or getting copied. Relationships are hard to duplicate.

**Reason #6: Low Cost** – With the right referral marketing system, you won't spend money on expensive advertising. The cost is very low for referral marketing. Even with a Referral Reward Program (which I highly recommend), the cost is still extremely low compared to most advertising.

**Reason #7: High Returns** – The returns can potentially be huge. In many industries a 4-to-1 return on investment on advertising dollars would be outstanding. In other words, if you invested $1000.00 in advertising, you would get an average of $4000.00 in return. With referral marketing, if you pay a 10% referral reward and everyone cashes in on it, you will have a 10-to-1 return. In my reward program, I get a 20-to-1 return.

**Reason #8: Returns Guaranteed** – With a referral reward, you don't pay it until *after* the product or service is paid for. With traditional advertising, you put your money on the line and hope for a return.

**Reason #9: Small Time Investment** – The biggest objection I get to referral marketing is "time." See Reason #10 to overcome that challenge.

**Reason #10: EXPO-NEN-TIAL MULTIPLI-CATION!!**

Would you be interested in how investing just a few minutes a day doing something really fun would give you a return of over $10,000.00 in new business each and every month after six months? Of course you would. Even though I can't guarantee it, I have seen it happen many times.

Here's what I discovered with referral marketing (see chart on next page).

# Exponential Multiplication Chart

☐ New Income    ■ Recurring Income    ■ Total Income

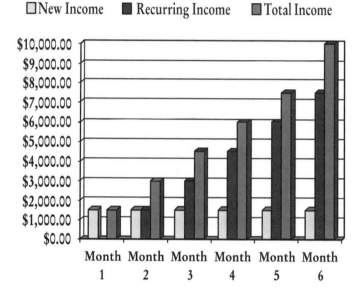

If you invest just 30 minutes per day calling on powerful referral sources (companies that are in a position to refer you on a regular basis), do you think it's possible to generate just $1,500.00 in new referrals in a one-month period? (See the light gray column on the chart.) Not too difficult for most small businesses.

What I discovered about referral marketing is that once you win the confidence of a referral source, they will continue the habit of referring you (the light gray column), unless you give them a reason not to. You will then continue to develop new referral sources each month to the tune of $1,500.00 each month.

All told, at the end of six months you would be at over $10,000.00 per month in NEW referred business! The total monthly income in new business is demonstrated by the second, darker column.

This is how I built my first company from the trunk of my car to a consistent $2.5 million per year. This is how I built a powerful training business, and it is the same method I have taught countless small business owners to use around the world. It will work for you, too.

Your referral marketing system should include: Consistent networking, referral source visits, mailers, and e-mails at minimum. There are also a number of phenomenal joint ventures, events and strategies that are amazing. To learn more about my Phenomenal Referral Marketing Systems, contact Phenomenal Products.

**3. Get More Sales from Existing Clients.**

## The Lifetime Client Marketing System -
## How to DOUBLE YOUR BUSINESS
## *without adding a single customer!*

The biggest marketing mistake of all is *not marketing to your existing client base*. Those who have already spent money with you. Did you know that statistics reveal it costs 500% more to gain a new client than to keep an existing one? Did you also know that without consistent marketing, many of your clients forget to call you and eventually end up using someone else?

It's a hard fact to swallow, but it's true.

A multi-industry study by The Wharton School of Business, University of Pennsylvania, revealed that companies who increased their customer retention rate by a mere 5 to 11 percentage points actually increased their profits by an astounding 25 to 75 percent, depending on the industry!

Back in 1999 I was mailing four times per year to my client base. That kept my repeat rate (something you need to be tracking) consistent. I wondered what would happen if I increased the number of mailings to 12. The investment was around $20K, but the *trackable* return was over $200K in the first year! It is my experience that many companies can double their business in the next 12 months without actually adding a single customer.

## *Five Critical Reasons to Market to Your Client Base*

1. **Get a higher price.** One of the reasons to constantly be in front of your past and existing clients (other than the fact that your competitor is marketing to them), is to reinforce your brand message, which positions you at a higher value. Translation: Higher price. Constantly remind them of the reasons to always use you and build the unique experience around your company.

2. **T.O.M.A. (Top Of Mind Awareness).** Just because you did a great job doesn't mean your customers will remember you. I had six thousand dollars' worth of plumbing done in my commercial building. I completely forgot about the plumber that services my home. Why? Because he doesn't have a system to stay in touch. Do you? How many of your customers are gone because of it?

3. **Sell more products and services.** You probably have a variety of products and services in addition to your "main" product

or service. Marketing to your past clients can dramatically increase your income and profit margin!

4. **Increase frequency of use.** Getting your clients to purchase more often is another powerful thing that can add lots of dollars to your business.

5. **Referrals!** If your client has trouble remembering your name, much less all the wonderful things that set you apart, what are the chances they are going to be a good referral source? A strong client-based marketing program can dramatically increase your referrals, especially if you have a referral reward program.

Your client-based marketing system should include regular mailers,

e-mails, thank you cards or letters, surveys, referral cards and phone calls. To learn more about our Phenomenal Client-Based Marketing Systems, contact Phenomenal Products.

## *Phenomenal Direct Marketing*

I try to avoid paid advertising and cold calling if I can. I would much rather do referral marketing, and if you have a client base, by all means market to them first. However, direct marketing does work if you understand it and apply it properly (like everything else).

### *The things I feel are important are found in the Four M's of Marketing...*

The first "M" is your target *Market*. You must understand who your niche market is. Know as much about demographics (gender, age, geography) and psychographics (lifestyle and their buying behavior) as possible.

The second "M" is your *Message*. Now that you understand your market, what are their needs? What are their desires? What are their fears? If you look at the advertising of most small businesses, it doesn't answer the most basic of questions...

"Why should I choose you over someone else?"

Having a message that shares what your unique benefits are is important. Then there is a great deal to learn about writing copy. I don't have the time or space to cover that in this book, but contact Phenomenal Products and we'll help you with that.

But you must have a compelling message and copy that causes them to respond. Once you get good at developing copy, you will be able to get a bigger response in all that you do. It's a very valuable skill.

The third "M" is *Method.* Does the method of advertising (or marketing) reach your target market? It does you no good to advertise to the wrong prospects.

The fourth "M" is *Money.* Is the advertising vehicle able to generate enough profit for you? In other words, if you invest $2,000.00 on an ad, and your cost of doing business is 50%, you will have to do $4,000.00 in business just to break even. You should track the ROI of all of your marketing efforts.

## *Phenomenal Internet Marketing*

I find the small business world in a very interesting place when it comes to online marketing. On the one hand, you have small business owners that are still confused about how it all works and the SEO-telemarketer-of-the-day telling you how they can get you on the first page of Google. At the same time, you have a generation that dismisses anything that isn't digital as old-school, slow and ineffective.

The truth is in the middle (as usual). How you use the Internet really depends on your target market and what you are selling, but here are a few rules that I think cross all lines...

1. Have at least one website (on a blog platform so you can manage it yourself).

2. Use a branded e-mail address that has your branding domain in it. Example: howard@ howardpartridge.com. Using a Gmail, AOL, or yahoo e-mail to communicate with business associates devalues your brand. Having your website address present encourages people to visit your site. Also, have at least your contact info in your e-mail signature (address, phone, website, etc.), and maybe even an opt-in...

3. Have a compelling opt-in on your site (free report, discount, etc.) so that you can build an e-mail list.

4. Have a regular outgoing e-mail newsletter. Just like client-based marketing, this educates and brands your business so you can take up the slot you want.

5. Have a social media presence at minimum, and respond to messages and friend requests.

The degree to which you use social media, SEO, e-mail and other forms of Internet advertising will depend on a lot of factors. If you are one of those still "confused" about it all, you cannot remain that way. Get educated. NOW. Then you can make an educated decision about how much you should use it. If you are of the "younger" generation that doesn't know what "snail mail" is, you might want to broaden your horizons, too!

## *Direct Sales*

Finally, there's the age-old idea of actually making a sales call! Part marketing and part sales, direct sales is when you market directly to a prospect in person. Don't discount this process! I mentioned network marketing in the previous chapter, which is a form of direct sales.

The fact that you are taking the time to speak to ONE person is not the issue; it's what can happen as a result. In the case of network marketing, for example, this person could build a huge team for you in the future. Perhaps it's a person who can become a monthly recurring client for you. My wife is in radio advertising sales. Outside of calling on ad agencies that she is assigned to, she has to actually CALL on someone! Imagine that! To be effective in direct sales, you first have to give them a compelling reason to meet with you. You and I both get solicitations every day for some kind of advertising. The problem is most of them are lame. Give your prospect something of value...a free trial, a free report, education, candy, gum, donuts, SOMETHING! But don't just call me up to sell me something without sharing what's in it for me (WIIFM).

In my companies, I always try to add value to the presentation. "Here's what you are going to get as a result of our time together." Make sense?

Once you make a presentation, ask for the sale (in the right way, of course). If you believe in your product or service, you shouldn't have any problem doing that. Finally, the fortune is in the follow-up. I can't tell you how many people I would have bought from who never called back!

The ultimate is to put them into a "forever follow-up system" that includes follow-up mail, calls, and e-mails. You can automate all of this with software and it doesn't have to be you doing any of it. You just have to develop the system that works.

To learn the techniques of how to do this, contact Phenomenal Products.

# Pillar #2:
# SALES

"Sales" is everything you do to turn a prospect into a paying *customer*. This includes answering the phone, your phone scripts, responding to an e-mail opt-in, presentations and so on. Once they have actually purchased something from you, they are now a customer.

Many times you may not need more prospects, but you need to take better care of the leads you get. Is your phone answered live? Is your phone answered in the most professional way possible? Do prospects and clients have a great experience when they call your company? Are your closing ratios what they need to be? Do you consistently make the add-on sale?

Do you have proven scripts for your people to follow so that you aren't the only one that can close the "big deals"? Do you have phenomenal on-site sales materials? How effective is your response to Internet leads? Increasing your closing ratios and your job averages can have a big impact on your business.

## *How to Double Your PROFIT with One Simple, Easy Strategy...*

In any business there is one type of sale that brings the most profit. There is one single sales activity that can make the most difference in the profitability of your company.

**<u>Not taking advantage of this all-important sales opportunity will cost you thousands of dollars.</u>**

That sale is called the "add-on" sale. The reason this type of sale is so profitable is because you have already invested the cost of acquiring and serving your client. Therefore, anything that is added to the "ticket" is extremely profitable. This makes the add-on sale the most profitable sale you can make.

With that said, how do we add on more sales? And more important, why don't YOU make the add-on sales that you "should" be making? The actual techniques of up-selling are not that difficult or tricky, but there is a deeper issue that must be addressed.

The deeper issue has to do with overcoming fear (remember the definition of fear? False Evidence Appearing Real). Many times we are afraid to ask for an extra sale. We feel like the client will get upset. They will think we are too pushy. They will see us as a "used-car-salesman" type.

You certainly want to be sensitive in the way you ask for the add-on product or service. But prepare to be SHOCKED – do you realize you are actually doing your customer a DISSERVICE by not offering the additional services? You should also be shocked at the amount of money you are leaving on the table.

The add-on sale benefits:

1. You (or your company)

2. Your employee

3. Your client

Let's look at you first. What's the value of an add-on sale? Just a small amount of $50.00 per day average in add-on sales five days a week totals up to **$13,000.00 per year.** If you had three employees, that's **$39,000.00** in additional income that goes to the company. One of my companies averages $300K in add-on sales per year. I want you to think about your life goals and what kind of impact add-on sales would have.

Now let's talk about your employee. If your employee has a financial incentive, it's pretty easy to show them the math. The big reason they don't up-sell is because they haven't been expected to or trained to do it. One of my employees made an additional $3,485.00 this past month just in his add-on bonuses.

Some business owners don't believe in giving incentives for add-on sales because they feel that it may tempt an employee to use high pressure or to be unethical. I have proven that if you build the right culture in your business and you don't tolerate high pressure, you can have a good balance.

Whether or not you decide to offer your employee a financial incentive, here's the biggest reason they should make the add-on sale...not doing so is an injustice to your client!

How could they possibly benefit from buying more from you? Obviously, the benefit of having the service or product is there, and I am hopeful you believe that much in your product. But more important than the benefit is the potential loss to the client if they do not get the product or service.

What is the actual, realistic, potential loss your client may experience by not purchasing the add-on? Are you completely convinced that this extra item will benefit your client? If so, aren't they going to miss out on that?

To add insult to injury, you don't offer the add-on and next thing you know, your client is buying the product from your most despicable competitor!!! Understand that by offering a great add-on service you are doing your clients a favor. You are helping them, not hurting them.

There are more sales techniques and concepts than I could begin to mention here, but asking questions is a good start. Simply noticing a need and letting them know about a product or service is a start. Of course, demonstrations, free trials, and presentations can take it to the next level.

A final note…don't offer *anything* until you have established a rapport with the client and you have secured *believability.* You must establish yourself as a trusted consultant and representative before attempting an extra sale. Many times this is accomplished by WOWing the client with the primary service or product first.

## The Phenomenal 7- Step Sales System

I developed a powerful sales system that I use in both of my companies very effectively. One of the most important things in sales is asking questions. Here I will share my steps with you in an article of mine that was published about asking questions.

## "May I Ask You a Question?"

*Do you know about the "power of the question"?*

*Did you know that "tellin' ain't sellin"?*

*Have you heard that asking questions during a sales presentation is much more effective than talking about your product or service? Have you noticed that most salespeople break that rule on a regular basis? The last time you bought something, did the salesperson ask good questions or did he/she do most of the "telling"?*

*What about you? How are you doing in that area? Have you practiced the skill of asking questions? Have you discovered the power behind asking the right questions?*

*In fact, have you discovered the right questions to ask for your industry? Would you be surprised to find out that the questions are very similar for any product or service?*

*What are the best questions to ask?*

*What about asking a new prospect...*

*"Who do I have the pleasure of speaking with today?"*

*(By the way, have you heard that someone's name is music to their ears?)*

*Wouldn't it be a good idea to use their name along with all of the following questions that are directed toward them?*

*"How were you referred to us?"*

*"What prompted you to call us instead of someone else?"*

*"What did (the person or company that referred them) say about us?"*

*Or..."What was it about the ad/letter/etc., that got your attention?"*

*Do you think asking those questions might give you insight into their reasons for choosing you?*

*You don't want to miss that, right?*

*What if you followed that with...*

*"Would you mind if I share a little bit about how we do things here and how we can be of benefit to you?"*

*What if you then took about 60 seconds to share how you can help them solve the major challenges that you know they have, based on your industry research?*

*Do you think this might help you connect with them emotionally and to position yourself as the credible source?*

*Have you crafted a compelling USP (Unique Selling Proposition) that will accomplish that?*

*Is it memorized or somewhere you can access it whenever you might happen to speak to a prospect?*

*What if you then followed that with a series of pre-planned questions that would not only help you discover their needs, but help them to discover what their true needs are, also?*

*Did you know that most people don't really understand what their true need is and how not solving it is hurting them worse than they realize?*

*Do you think you could improve on the questions you ask?*

*What if you followed the discovery questions with some possible solutions, but you put the solutions in the form of a question?*

*What questions could you follow a statement with?*

*What about, "Does that make sense?"*

*Or, "Does that sound like what you are looking for?"*

*Did you know that by slowing down and asking confirming questions that you can uncover more objections than you would by just running through your benefits?*

*Did you realize that by getting them to say "yes" throughout the process, that they will be more likely to say "yes" when you share the investment?*

*What if you could overcome all objections before you quoted the investment?*

*How cool would that be?*

*By the way, what do you do when you get an objection?*

*What if you asked a question?*

*What kind of question?*

*What about, "What do you mean, 'it's too high'?"*

*Does it make sense that when you simply repeat the objection, they are likely to tell you what the real objection is?*

*Have you heard that when you quote the investment, the first person to speak is usually the one who buys?*

*Do you make it a habit of becoming silent after quoting the investment?*

*If not, is it because you simply have not disciplined yourself, haven't understood the importance until now, or is it because you don't believe in your price?*

*Finally, does it make sense that getting really good at asking good questions will help you sell more?*

*And how will selling more benefit you?*

*Did you notice that there isn't one single statement in this article?*

## Pillar #3:
## OPERATIONS

Once the customer has purchased, everything that happens to serve that customer is operations. This includes your delivery. The level of service you provide will determine whether they will ascend the loyalty ladder and go from customer to *client*.

Do you have service systems in place so that your clients get *the* most outstanding service experience *ever*, consistently, *every* time, without you having to be personally involved?

To take this area to the next level, you want to first think about what kind of service experience you want your clients, members or patients to have. The level of service experience will determine how much you can charge.

I learned a great way to think about this from my colleague Ellen Rohr. Think about the process of serving a customer from their eyes. Put yourself in their shoes and walk through the experience as they would.

The example she gave was a restaurant. Get in the car and drive down the road toward the restaurant. Can you see the sign? Is the light on? Is it easy to park? Is the parking lot clean?

Now approach the building. Is it inviting? Is the front door clean or does it need a little Windex? Is the hostess missing? I think you get the picture – at each step, what could go WRONG?

Now, simply take that list and work out the service experience. For a service company, it begins with the A.M. procedures. Are the trucks washed, stocked and ready? Do we have a system for that? Are the techs in uniform and ready to go? Do they have their client info? Create a checklist for the day and begin working on your systems so that you can not only provide the most outstanding service experience, but so that you can also duplicate it over and over, regardless of who is in each position.

The subtitle of *The Experience Economy* (Joseph Pine and James Gilmore) is *Work is Theatre and Every Business is a Stage*. What is theatre? It's an experience designed to create an emotional response. Will they laugh or cry? So, putting your service experience together is much like a theatre production.

## Pillar #4:
## ADMINISTRATION

The final pillar is the tracking piece. This is your financial statements, marketing results, your production rates, your sales closing rates and everything else that needs to be tracked to confirm that you are profitable and efficient.

Do you know what your cost of doing business is? Do you know what your marketing efforts are producing? Do you know what your sales closing rates are? Do you know what your production rates are? Do you have a written business plan?

Do you have a budget for the next 12 months? Do you have the right insurance and legal protection? Most people are not really savvy when it comes to bookkeeping, tracking software, and things that can make this pillar really strong. Learn the numbers. Learn technology. It will do you good.

Most small businesses I come across can use a lot of help in all of these areas, but I have also found that most small business owners are strong in one particular area (usually operations) and not so much on the other parts. So, to build a better, stronger business, start with assessing each pillar to determine how you are doing in each area. Think about each area in your business.

To learn more about these processes and to get proven systems and support for your business, contact Phenomenal Products.

### *The other "7" in the 747 business model...*

The third digit in 747 is for the **7 Steps of Implementation**:

1. **Inspiration – Get Fired Up!** The first step in overcoming F.T.I. (Failure To Implement) is to stay inspired. Are you constantly exposing yourself to information that inspires you? Do you have a community to support you? If you aren't inspired, you won't act.

For me, beginning my day reading a chapter from the Bible and investing a few minutes reading from a business book or magazine keeps me inspired. When I see what other people have done, it motivates me. I listen to praise and worship music while I work and CDs by Zig Ziglar and other phenomenal trainers while driving. I avoid negative conversations (unless I'm the one complaining! LOL!).

2. **Quick-Start – Get Things Moving NOW!** What are the immediate action steps you can take to get your business moving in the right direction? There are probably things you KNOW you should be doing. If you are not inspired, get going on those things right now. To make absolutely sure you are always working on the biggest return-on-investment items, make sure you have a support group that KNOWS business, so you can stay focused, accountable and inspired.

3. **Tracking – Where You Are Now**. This is the weakest link in so many small businesses. Success is defined by whether they are *busy* or not. The sad fact is that you can be *busy* and *broke!* If you want to work smarter rather than harder, learn how to

run your stats. If you are traveling in a vehicle, how do you know whether you have enough gas to reach your destination? The gas gauge, of course! How do you know if your oil is low? Have you done regular maintenance to make sure your tires and belts are in good shape? Get the picture? You're driving blind! As it is often said in the training world, "If you can't measure it you sure can't manage it!"

4. **Goals – Where You Want To Go**. Once you have determined where you are, you can better plan your mile-markers. What are the stats you want to improve? By how much? Keep your goals very specific and measurable. Have a deadline and write it down.

5. **Plans – How You Will Get There**. Now you want to really focus on what strategies you will use. There are literally hundreds of strategies you could implement. The problem is that most small business owners have no direction other than to put out the brush fire or react to not being *busy*. If you take the time and work the 747 business model, you not only have a better chance of reaching the success you desire, but you are now in a position that very few

will ever be able to be in – a position to have a turnkey business.

6. **Systems – How You Will Stay There.** Systems is the key to a predictable, profitable turnkey operation. Once you take action on your plans, you find out what works, what doesn't, what you want to tweak, and you end up with...a system! This is how we do it here! Just duplicate it over and over again.

7. **Leadership – Getting Others To Help You.** If you want to do truly phenomenal things in your business, you really can't do it by yourself. But you may have bought into the LIE that you can't find good people. If you have employees, do you have to tell them over and over what to do? Do you know how to properly coach an employee back to performance? Do you know the right way to terminate someone? <u>Your employees are your greatest asset or your biggest nightmare, and that depends mostly on your leadership skills.</u>

Like everything else I have shared in this book so far, this is a skill anyone can learn. If your dream is important to you, I suggest

you learn this skill. One of the most grati-
fying parts of my life is training leaders –
watching them grow as they grow people.

# 5

## YOUR PHENOMENAL BODY

A few years ago, night after night I would come home to repeat the same routine. Famished from a busy day that started with too much Starbucks coffee and no breakfast, I would consume everything I could find.

Overweight and lethargic, I whined to my wife. She replied with, "I think your hormones are off."

I thought to myself, "What's a hormone? Don't just women have those?" (I told you I'm from Alabama!) Turns out she was right. Not only was I overweight and out of shape, but my hormones were off the charts.

I found that out by consulting a certified nutritionist who began to paint a very bleak picture of my future. Chances are I wouldn't just drop dead of an instant heart attack, but I would end up like so many Americans – shuffling around with a myriad of diseases – surviving on medication.

And THAT, my friend, is NOT very phenomenal!

The eventual result of visiting that nutritionist was a loss of 50 pounds. At that time, I also had terrible migraines. It would not be unusual to have a migraine once a week. Many years ago, my wife and I were on a trip to Holland and I had one of the worst migraines ever – to the point that I actually threw up. A Dutch guy stopped to help and directed us to what he thought was a doctor's office. It turned out to be a veterinarian! However, with socialized medicine, he was able to give me a prescription! How many of us can say we've been treated by a vet! Not sure if that is something to be proud of or not!

Once I began eating healthy foods, the migraines I suffered from for years were gone! (Of course, it doesn't take a genius to figure out that if you don't eat breakfast, you drink a lot of coffee, you barely eat lunch and then you gorge on everything from pickles to ice cream all night, you're likely to wake up with a headache!)

The specifics of my eating plan really aren't even important because they may be different for you. Go find a phenomenal nutritionist and let a professional prescribe a plan for you.

Here's what's MOST important...

It was the PICTURE I got as the nutritionist painted a picture of my probable future. The picture was depressing. The picture of my demise - a picture of the worst situation I could possibly imagine myself in – crippled and broken down.

Now, don't get me wrong. If you are in that position because of a disease or an accident, that's one thing; but to be in a wheelchair because we ate too much white bread and sugar is different. And that's where most of us Americans live. We either don't know any better or we don't have power to overcome it.

The picture the nutritionist painted was compelling. That's what a good coach or consultant does

– they help you SEE. The picture of desperation, along with the sluggish feeling I already had, was enough to make me change. The best part is that soon after implementing her prescription, I began getting inspired. Now I began seeing the picture of a thin, strong, fit Howard. And the result always follows the clear picture. Always.

I began playing basketball weekly and I hired a trainer twice a week. I got really strong. I could do 50 push-ups (before that I probably would have struggled with three!). I never saw myself as a "health nut" and people who ate organic foods were just plain *weird*. But as I became aware of how many of the foods we eat are like poison to our bodies, I now focus on eating all natural foods.

If you want to get fit, you have to change your picture. You must realize what the result of staying unhealthy will ultimately be. No denial; face reality. Until you do that, no technique will help you.

For me, my prescription included having some protein and fruit in the morning. Lunch and dinner is a small portion of lean meat (or beans), vegetables and fruit. That's it.

People are also surprised to learn that I get a lot of sleep. I normally sleep 7-8 hours a night, and in the afternoons I'll typically take a short 30-minute "siesta" outside by the pool or on the beach if I'm in Florida. I produce a lot and I guess people assume that I do it by burning the candle. Quite the contrary. Not only do I go to bed by 9 or 10 p.m., I rarely work after 6 p.m. I might check e-mail on my phone or do some social networking on my iPad, but my work day is very structured, and I have systems and staff so that I can focus on projects that will move the ball down the field. I mostly work "on" the business instead of in it. Of course, there is the occasion when I'm traveling and I have to rise at 4 a.m. to catch an early flight, but I probably went to bed at 9 p.m., so even that doesn't hurt that much.

I also learned that getting a massage on a regular basis is very healthy. Of course, that's not cheap, so you've got to make some phenomenal money or make friends with a massage therapist! I drink a lot of water, too.

I had lived like this for about five years and was downright militant about it. Then I got bored with my strength training. I wished it could be as much fun as basketball. It was expensive, too, so I fired my trainer, fooling myself into thinking I would diligently work out on my own. How do you think that went? NOT!

The result was my legs weren't as strong as they were when I was training twice a week, and when

I play basketball, I'm like the Tasmanian Devil. I play EXTREME basketball. I blew out my knee. I had a torn cartilage and meniscus disc. Plus, I had some arthritis behind the kneecap. My post-surgery rehab prevented impact, so basketball was out for five months.

During the time of inactivity, I lost my vision on my eating plan and I gained 25 pounds back. Still eating fairly healthily, and still looking good (my wife and others thought I looked too thin at 165), I began to slowly allow unhealthy things back into my diet.

Every year I have to do an online health assessment to qualify for a better rate on our health insurance. It asks you a number of questions and rates your health. During that one year, I declined from *super healthy* to *average* health.

Average is not phenomenal. And that was unacceptable. Once I was able to get back to physical activity, I rehired my trainer and I am at basketball weekly. My picture began to return.

Here's a very important point: I noticed a correlation between the clarity of my picture and my support system. I rarely talked to my nutritionist after awhile. In all seven areas of life, we need a community of people to support us and to help us keep our picture. I have found this is the key. Support. Community.

Community is what keeps alcoholics sober. It's what keeps believers built up, and it's what keeps one another inspired. When you are inspired, you can do anything.

So, take some time to think about your physical condition. Build a picture of the person you want to be. Perhaps you currently smoke and you want to be a non-smoker. Visualize that and build a support community around you to keep you encouraged and focused.

# 6

# PHENOMENAL
# FAMILY RELATIONSHIPS

At a dinner celebrating my wife's parents' 50th anniversary, someone asked them what their secret was. They looked at each other and shrugged their shoulders. Like an excited schoolboy who knew the answer, I piped up with "I know." I had been watching them all these years (wondering what the secret was myself), and I realized they were simply unselfish. Today, our problem in America is that it's all about us. We want others to change and conform to our specifications of what the relationship should look like.

I don't know about you, but I have realized that you can't change anyone. When you try, the result is a broken relationship or you tolerate the other person rather than having the kind of relationship you should have. It could be that the other person may never change, but you can be successful in this area by being who *you* are supposed to be. Would you agree that if you do that there is much more of a chance of them changing? If you are waiting for someone else to be or do something before you are all you need to be, you have already lost the battle. Let go of the ego and forgive them.

In cases of abuse and/or addictions that are destroying the family, get professional help. This book is for those that are somewhat functional. It isn't for severe cases, although it will help anyone who is willing to change.

I can truly say that at this moment, my relationship with my wife is better than ever after 27 years of marriage. It wasn't always that way. In the early years of our marriage, I had a terrible marijuana addiction that drove her crazy! After 12 years of it, I came to know the Lord; I was delivered instantly. It was a miracle. You can read more about that in my Spiritual testimony. I later learned that many addicts spend the rest of their lives in the "recovery" community, staving off the next temptation. I was free in an instant, which is unusual, so I know that it was God.

I jumped straight from that addiction to becoming the biggest zealot Christianity had ever seen. I felt so free that I wanted everyone to have what I had. I think that's in my DNA. I began to follow my wife around the house with a Bible, telling her she needed to get saved or she was going to hell. After several months of preaching at her, she finally responded with, "Look, I might be Catholic and stupid, but I do know this...Jesus was a single man and if you want to be like Him that can be arranged!"

I thought to myself, "Somehow this isn't working." So I decided to keep my mouth shut and serve her instead. Someone once said, "Preach the gospel. Use words if necessary." I took the garbage out and unloaded the dishwasher. I began to diligently take care of my responsibilities as a husband. Before too long my wife came to know the Lord and is a powerful witness for Him today.

At this writing, my son is 18 and on his way to Texas Tech University. He is a fine young man with a huge heart for people. Our relationship today is really good, but it wasn't always that way. When he was younger, I demanded absolute obedience from him. I said "no" more than "yes," it seemed. We endured many heart-wrenching trials, and at a point not too awfully long ago, my relationship with him was a "2" on the Wheel of Life. Today, I would put it at a borderline eleven! We love each other very much. You see, when I changed, he changed. I don't like to live with regrets, but I can't help think of what could have been possible had I approached him differently as he was growing up.

I certainly don't want to be the one to make you feel bad about a strained relationship, but I do want to be the one to wake you up while there is still time. I want you to know that the possibilities are grander than you could ever imagine, if you are willing to swallow some pride and you're willing to change.

The place to start is to simply stop trying to convince the other person to see things your way. At the same time, if you have worthy goals and people close to you who like to throw cold water on your dreams, just keep those dreams to yourself. Share them with your Dream Team. Begin to simply be gracious and kind. Employ the "Golden Rule" of "doing to others as you would have them do you." This also goes for people who treat you badly.

Remember that those who are close to you that don't support your dream may doubt, based on past experiences. If your dream will affect them, they will have to leave their comfort zone. They may have to fail with you to reach success, and they may not be ready for it. Also realize that "hurt people hurt people." When someone is hurting, they will lash out at you because they have such a poor self-image. This was the case with my son. I was shocked to learn how he saw himself, because as his dad, I knew how smart and how talented he was.

When people have a poor self-image, they will act that out as we have learned already in this book. I never wanted to learn about human behavior. I just wanted to serve people and make them happy. But what I have learned is that all of life is about relationships and all of business is about relationships. And to understand relationships, you have to have some understanding of human behavior.

So, when you begin to understand before being understood (one of Steven Covey's *7 Habits of Highly Successful People*), you might be surprised to see the tide turn. If there has been a lot of hurt, it might take a while. You may need professional help. But I'm here to tell you that it is possible, and you will be a better, happier person if you do your part. Your mind will then be unlocked to receive the inspiration and creativity that comes from a joyful mind. Love is the opposite of selfishness. Love is not a feeling but a commitment. The problem today is that we aren't willing to sacrifice.

The person you become when you endure trials and tribulations is one who has great character and experiences that you can share with others. The internal pain and emptiness that come from "copping out" last much longer than any short-lived relief you might feel. Zig Ziglar says, "The chief cause of unhappiness is trading what you want most (a great long-term relationship, in this case) for what you want now (your emotional need to be right). I suppose this is why our society is so sour today. We have literally spoiled ourselves. What we want most is meaningful relationships, yet we have traded that for the desire of the moment. It's never too late. Whatever the strained family relationship may be, you be the phenomenal one and take the first step toward peace.

# 7

# I AM

Warning! This chapter includes information about Jesus Christ. If that subject offends you, you may not want to read this chapter. While I do not wish to push my faith on you, I would be remiss if I did not share the most important part of my life.

If you are in the media, or you hire me to speak, you do not have to worry about me "preaching" to your audience. My reputation proves that.

However, if you are from the community of faith, there is nothing I love to talk about more than God.

So, please proceed with that understanding and as the old saying goes, "last but not least" is an understatement in this case. In fact, this is the most important chapter of the entire book. I would be remiss if I shared how to be phenomenally successful in life without acknowledging the "Giver of Life." This chapter is about the spiritual aspects of our lives.

As I said in the beginning of the book, you were *created* to be phenomenal. First, you were *created*. You were created to *be*. To be phenomenal. After all, "God don't make no junk!"

Notice that I said the "spiritual" aspects of our lives, not the "religious" aspects of our lives. There's a difference. If you are not a follower of Jesus Christ, you may have been turned off by "Christian religion," which is *not* what I am talking about.

Christianity is a faith.

It's a faith that Jesus Christ is the one and only Son of God. That He is the Truth, the Way and the Life, and that no man comes to the Father but through Him (Jesus' words). You may not believe in Jesus. You may be of another religion or faith. This entire book is simply about sharing my philosophies of life with you. My prayer is that Jesus would reveal Himself to you so that you can know Him, which will give you His Holy Spirit that will give you power here on earth and will give you eternal life.

When you look at the Wheel of Life, the order of importance of the spokes is really Spiritual, then Family, because I don't believe you can lead your family properly if you aren't right spiritually. And no amount of personal success or business success can compensate for failure at home. After family would probably come Physical health, because if you don't have your health, you are limited in the other areas.

You might put Mental after that because the more you know how to use your mind, the more successful you will be in your Career. And the better you do in your Career will determine how your Financial spoke rates. Finally, your Financial spoke determines the amount of funding you have for the Personal spoke.

So it looks like this in the order of importance:

1. Spiritual

2. Family

3. Physical

4, Mental

5. Career

6. Financial

7. Personal

This chapter is titled "I AM" in CAPITAL letters because when Moses went up to Mount Sinai to meet God he asked Him what His name was so that he could tell those at the bottom of the mountain about Him. He said tell them, "I AM Who I AM." When Jesus made a statement to the religious people of the day about seeing Abraham, they asked how he could have possibly known Abraham who lived hundreds of years before. Jesus responded with, "Before Abraham was, I AM."

Those two words are probably the most powerful two words in the English language. The reason? It brings us full circle to where we started: Your identity. Your image of yourself, God and the world. Most Christians don't know WHO they are in Christ. The I AM that created the heavens and the earth is IN YOU.

Now, that's amazing.

When I first came to know the Lord, I didn't know who I was. I was a religious zealot. When you come to realize that Christ IN YOU is the hope of glory, and that it was for freedom's sake you have been set free, and that Christ wants to live through you, this is where you get freedom. You must know who you are in Christ.

This is the most important subject of your life, so if you want to find out who you are (or who you can be), begin to understand who you are in Christ. Bill and Annabel Gillham have a wonderful product called "The Life" that will assist you in your search.

As for me, I'll just share what happened to me on my spiritual journey. Before I share my personal testimony, I want to share how God was in the creation of Phenomenal Products. I think after reading the following paragraphs that you will understand why you could never convince me that Jesus isn't alive and real right now today. Too much has happened in my life. At first, I believed by faith. Now He has demonstrated His existence and His power in my life. That's how it works. You believe by faith and He is faithful and true to do exceedingly abundantly more than you could ever ask, think or imagine!

### *Proverbs 15:22*

When I launched Phenomenal Products in 1998, my service company had just done over $1 million in revenue for the first time. I got the vision to write a few manuals. At that time, I still had to be at the office around 7:30 in the morning. I had two partners, but we had just joined together 18 months prior and there were still many obligations to tend to. But I had this vision of Phenomenal Products.

So, I started getting up at 3 or 4 in the morning to work on these manuals. I would write for two to three hours and then go down to the shop. After about six weeks of this, it occurred to me that I hadn't prayed about it. So, I stopped to pray and I felt that God gave me Proverbs 15:22 that says, "Without consultation, plans are frustrated, but with many counselors, plans succeed."

I thought to myself, "This is really great. It fits." If you happen to have some of my early manuals, you will notice that Scripture on the cover.

I began selling the manuals and got even busier with Phenomenal Products. I found myself in Palm Springs, California, at a trade show. I had been gone for a week and I spent a lot of money on the event. I was coming back from Starbucks (I had one of those huge containers of Starbucks coffee in my booth that kept a steady flow of people coming by!).

I was doubting whether I had made the right move or not and I felt the Holy Spirit (not audibly) whisper, "Turn on the radio."

"I'm about to park," I argued.

"Turn on the radio."

"I don't have time," I retorted.

"Turn on the radio," The Holy Spirit insisted. So, I hit the button and the men on the station were talking about Proverbs 15:22! Confirmation #2.

A few more months went by and my partners were concerned because I wasn't participating in my service company to the level they felt that I should. I was torn between the two companies. As I was driving home one day I was wrestling with this in my mind. As I pulled into my driveway about dusk, I noticed that my next door neighbor (who was a pastor of a large church) had left the light on in his truck. I didn't want him to have to jump-start his battery the next morning, so I went over to tell him that he had left his light on.

We began talking and I shared with him what I was going through. By the way, he knew NOTHING about Phenomenal Products. We rarely talked and when we did, it was a casual greeting in passing. He began to quote Proverbs 15:22. Confirmation #3. That's when I knew that Phenomenal Products was not just a company that I wanted to start, but something God was prompting me to do for a greater purpose than just building a business.

And I have to say that the work that has been done at Phenomenal Products continues to help people worldwide. It has helped them with their businesses, their families, and even their faith. I'm just grateful to be a part!

So, to end this book I would like to share my spiritual testimony with you. Remember that you were created to BE a PHENOMENAL person, to DO PHENOMENAL things in the world, and to HAVE a PHENOMENAL L.I.F.E.

Live in Freedom Every Day.

In His Love,
Howard "Phenomenal" Partridge

# THE TRUE TESTIMONY OF HOWARD PARTRIDGE

It was a bitter, cold day in Houston, Christmas week of 1987. One of the slowest weeks of the year for my business. My three employees and I were getting high and listening to loud rock music. Mitch played along with his saxophone.  As I sat on the floor next to the couch, I felt that I had nothing to live for.

My wife and I did not get along because of my marijuana habit. She was visiting her parents in New Jersey at the time. The carpet cleaning business that

I had started three years prior was struggling. My friends were not much help, since most of them were potheads as well. I started smoking pot when I was 15 years old.

Until that point, I swore I would never touch it. But after trying it the first time, it was easier. Soon it became a daily habit and I did try other drugs along the way. None of the other drugs gripped me like marijuana. In 12 years it had become a love-hate relationship. A typical day for me would start with the thought of when I would be able to get high. I would get my work out of the way early in the day so that I could smoke without the bother of clients. Once I got high, I hated myself because I was unproductive and unmotivated.

The strangest thing happened in 1987. I began to get a feeling that my life was falling apart. I knew I had to quit smoking dope, but I couldn't. I also knew (or thought I knew) that life in general didn't excite me. Still I had this urge – almost like a warning – that I had to change. As this feeling grew stronger, I began to verbalize the fact that I needed to change. This unusual sense of urgency would not leave.

At the time, three of my friends worked for me. As we would get high together we all began to have the same feeling of a needed change. The odd thing is that in the midst of getting high, we shared with each other what we knew (or thought we knew) about God.

Before these conversations began, I knew deep down that the only answer to my problems lay somehow with God. When I was a boy, I attended an active Baptist church where I heard the Word often. I believed in my head and was even moved to be baptized at about age nine. However, God was not in my heart.

By the time I was in my early teens I began to skip church until, eventually, I didn't go anymore. So, deep down in my heart, I knew that I had to give my life to Jesus. Michael and I talked about it the most. He shared how he had walked with Christ for a year or so in Dallas and had then slipped back into his old ways. After a few weeks, the three of us had somehow entered into the conversations about God and Jesus.

This went on for a few weeks. We even got the Bible out on a couple of occasions. I can still remember one of them quoting a verse out of James. We all agreed that this was the way to go, but no one made a move. The uncomfortable feeling that I had still did not pass.

On that bitterly cold day in December of 1987, sitting on the floor, I remember thinking, "There has *got* to be more to life than this." I rose up and announced to the guys that I had decided to follow Jesus for real and to stop just talking about it. As I was about to leave I said, "I have decided to give my heart to Jesus. I am not going to smoke pot anymore."

I remember comments like, "Ha, ha, we'll see in a few days when you start craving for it." But at the instant that I made the decision and the confession, I felt like a changed man and to this day I haven't had even an inkling of a desire for marijuana again. After the first few days, I had an incredible feeling of a heavy burden being lifted from my shoulders. I could almost feel the absence of weight physically.

I remember the greatest thing was having my mind back. I know it may seem like a small thing for some people, but after 12 long years of living in an altered state of mind, not being able to think clearly or rationally, having that back is a big deal! I began to study the Bible furiously, and to shape my new-found faith. After about two weeks, two of my three employees came to know the Lord.

They are both fine Christian men today.

Many miracles have happened since then, most of which I will not mention, but a few I will. The first miracle was that my wife, who was in New Jersey at the time of my decision, had decided that she would not return if I had not changed. She had absolutely no indication that I would. The timing of God was incredible!

The second miracle that I will mention (there have been thousands) happened when I was in College Station, Texas. It was about 1989 and I was attending a gathering of churches. During a time of silent prayer for our own personal needs, each congregant was kneeling over their chair. I was praying about a particular matter, which I will not mention at present, but as I was praying, I felt a tremendously overwhelming sense that I was hearing in my soul the very words of God – although I didn't hear them audibly. I had never felt God's spirit so strongly.

Then I heard someone whisper my name (audibly) three times in a row, "Howard. Howard. Howard." I thought it was one of the ushers that needed my assistance. I looked up, but recognized that no one was near me. I heard it again. Again I looked around. Still I saw no one that I knew. Then I heard it a third time. It was then that I realized that this was the voice of God. I asked God if it was Him and I heard in my spirit, not audibly, "These things I want to confirm to you will come to pass." I could hardly sleep that night. It was one of the most moving things that ever happened to me. Seven years later, those issues that I was praying about came to pass.

The last miracle I would like to share concerns my father. My father and mother split up when I was about one year old. After two more daddies in my life, at the age of almost 18 I had a fight with my stepdad over my marijuana habit. We got into a little scuffle and the next day I was on a bus to Houston (from Mobile, Alabama, where I had grown up). My real father, whom I had only met twice in my life, lived in Houston, and I felt that he "owed" me, since he had never done anything for me (according to my mother). My sister (who I was very close to) was in Houston, living at my father's house.

Over the years my dad and I became very close, although each of us had large egos and many walls that kept us from sharing deeply. He was a difficult person to know intimately. However, he was very generous and helped me tremendously (I only had a quarter in my pocket upon my arrival in Houston). He bought me everything that I needed, even though I wasted so much. When I came to know Jesus, I longed to share the deep things of God with him. However, Earl Partridge was his own man. His personality, coupled with my inner feelings of wanting him to be proud of me (I struggled not to look foolish), made his acceptance very important to me.

My dad developed lung cancer. After fighting it for six years, he finally came to the obvious end. At this point I was not convinced that he knew God, even though he said he did. I struggled with how to share with him, and how to pray. My stepmother's sister, a fine Christian woman, told me that before her mother died, she prayed to God *specifically*, and He answered her prayers *specifically*.

That made good sense to me. I began to pray earnestly about four *specific* things: 1) That my dad would be saved. 2) That God would confirm it to me when he was saved. 3) That he would be healed. 4) That whenever he died, whether it be 10 weeks or 10 years from then, that God would allow me to be at his side.

As his health continued to deteriorate, the day came when the end was imminent. For weeks I had visited my dad daily. One Thursday I decided not to go because he'd had so many visitors in and out of the house lately. That Thursday night I got a call from my stepmother indicating I should come right away. I pleaded with the Lord to keep him alive until I got there. Upon arrival, he was still sitting up in his chair. We talked and cried together. However, I had an un-usual peace that he would not die that night, and that my prayers would still be answered.

The next day I came to his house about 10:30 in the morning and he was unconscious, but alive. His wife, Marie, and other son (my stepbrother, Lee) had not been able to raise him. He was kind of propped up in a chair. I began asking God, "What about my prayers? How will You possibly answer them now?"

I began to speak the name of Jesus into his ear. I told him that Jesus loved him very much and was preparing a special place for him. As I was speaking, he suddenly rolled his eyes up at me and in a rough, straining voice, spoke! "I didn't know you were here," he said.

He asked for a pad of paper and some ice. We fed him crushed ice for his dry mouth as he began to scribble, "I didn't know I was going to die until now. I have no more pain." He would collapse between words, as he didn't even have the strength to finish a sentence. "I am ready to go and be with *the Lord*," he wrote. He often referred to God as "the Lord," but rarely used the name Jesus. It was as though he was afraid of the name. Maybe that's why God told me to speak the name of Jesus in his ear.

After writing *"the Lord,"* he collapsed again. At that very moment, I felt a strong, vibrating voice go through my body that said, "He just gave his heart to Me. He will write the name *Jesus.*" And sure enough, he raised himself up and finished the sentence with *Jesus*!

"I am ready to go and be with the Lord, Jesus." He could have just written "the Lord" and everyone would have understood, but because God is rich in grace and mercy, and cares about our every need, He saw fit to do that miracle for me.

My dad died later that night and I was at his bedside. I have never shed more tears than I did as he breathed his last. Most of the tears were of sorrow that my dad was dead, but some were because of the awesome feeling that God had answered my prayers and that I would be spending eternity with my dad. God had answered miraculously all four of my requests. My stepbrother, Lee, was there, not quite realizing all that was taking place. A few years later, Lee gave his heart to the Lord, and I shared the experience with him.

If you don't know God, you are missing out on a life of love, peace, and miracles, missing eternal life with God. It is not enough to believe in God or to know *about* Him. John 17:3 reveals that as Jesus sweat blood in prayer to the Father, He said "This is eternal life, that they may know You, the only true God, and Jesus Christ whom You have sent."

That word *know* means to know Him *intimately*, not just from a distance. You must "know Him" intimately. The only way that can happen is for you to place your trust in Him so that He will reveal Himself to you.

*Howard Partidge*

# ABOUT THE AUTHOR

**Howard Partridge** grew up on welfare in Mobile Alabama and left home at 18. He arrived in Houston, Texas on a Greyhound bus with only 25 cents in his pocket.

At age 23, he started his first business out of the trunk of his car and built it up to a multi-million dollar enterprise. He has owned 8 small businesses altogether and owns 3 companies at the time of this printing.

He is president of Phenomenal Products, Inc. which helps small business owners stop being slaves to their business by transforming it into a predictable, profitable, turnkey operation.

For the past 15 years Howard has helped small business owners around the world dramatically improve their businesses. He currently has coaching members worldwide, is the exclusive small business coach for the Zig Ziglar corporation, is an independent, and a certified coach with the John C. Maxwell team.

Howard has led hundreds of seminars, webinars, workshops and holds his own live multi-day events which have featured some of America's top business trainers including Michael Gerber, Bob Burg, Dr. Joseph A. Michelli, and American legend Zig Ziglar.

Howard is married to Denise and has one beautiful son, Christian who is a freshman at Texas Tech University in Lubbock, Texas.

Get Free Videos, Webinars and Resources for growing a phenomenal business and living a phenomenal L.I.F.E. at **www.HowardPartridge.com**

# PHENOMENAL NOTES

# PHENOMENAL NOTES

# PHENOMENAL NOTES

# PHENOMENAL NOTES